Telling the Passenger Where to Get Off

Telling the Passenger

Where to Get Off

George Dow and the evolution of the railway diagrammatic map

Andrew Dow

FRSA

Capital Transport

For James and Alyx

so that they may know a little more of
the creativity of their grandfather.

By the same author
Norfolk & Western Coal Cars
Dow's Dictionary of Railway Quotations

Frontispiece: George Dow drawing a map in 1957.

Published by Capital Transport Publishing
PO Box 250, Harrow HA3 5ZU

© Andrew Dow 2005

Designed and typeset by Discript Ltd, London WC2N 4BN
Based on an original design by Justin Howes
Printed by Thomson Press, Lyon Road, Harrow HA1 2AG
ISBN 185414 291 7

Preface

This book has its origins in a handful of old carriage panel maps, which my father had kept for nearly sixty years since the late 1920s, and which came to me upon his death in 1987. He had several artefacts in his collection, many of which were items that represented railways that he admired, mementos from his career on the LNER and British Railways, and several books inscribed by grateful authors whom he had helped.

The maps were different, for he had created them himself. That fact alone did not draw my attention to them, for I had long known of his love of maps and his delight in drawing them. Why, I had even photographed him drawing maps for his trilogy, *Great Central*. Long had I watched him bent over his drawing board, sketching out and then inking in so carefully, and it seemed, so instinctively setting the layout and achieving the balance of an attractive map.

He did this before the easy availability of modern fountain drawing pens and certainly before any suggestion of drawing by computer. No, he created his maps the old way, with a fine-nibbed dip-it-in-the-bottle drawing pen and a pot of best Indian Ink. That, indeed, is how I learned engineering drawing from him and at school, first in pencil and then with the same rudimentary pen and ink.

It was with this sort of equipment that my father set himself the task, in early 1929, of preparing two carriage panel maps for the employer he had joined on 28 March 1927, the London & North Eastern Railway. The maps were his idea. The only record he made of their creation was that he had admired the way in which the Underground companies kept their passengers well informed, and that he felt sure that the LNER could do as well. And so having first obtained the measurements of the panels above the seatbacks of the standard LNER suburban stock, he drew maps of the GN and the GE lines.

They were not ordinary maps, for they were diagrammatic. The diagrammatic map was not a new device, for it had been slowly evolving on the railway for many years. But it had had limited use, and never before had entire systems been shown on a single diagrammatic map for public use. Their purpose was to provide information in a quickly digestible form, while the passenger was *en route*.

At the time he was attached to the Works Section within the Chief General Manager's office. He took the finished maps, offered them to the LNER, and they were accepted on the spot. At that moment seventy-five years ago, a little bit of railway history had been made. This book tells of the significance of those maps, and of the many others which my father created during the following twenty-five years of his railway career.

Andrew Dow

Newton-on-Ouse
October 2004

Acknowledgements

It is never possible to write a book such as this without the help of many people, and this book is no exception. Many collectors and people who have an abiding interest in maps, professional or otherwise, have helped me considerably, including particularly John Alsop, Roy Burrows, Richard Casserley, Tim Demuth, Stan Friedman, Dave Harris, Alan A Jackson, Peter Lloyd and Doug Rose.

Maxwell Roberts has spent much time carefully re-constructing two early route diagrams from information in old photographs. In the case of the District Railway map, he had only a blurred oblique image from which to work. He corrected the perspective electronically and then painstakingly overlaid a new map, following the lines and positions of stations of the original. The contents of the flags, giving connection data, were largely illegible or obscured, and these texts had to be researched at some length. All the work that he has done is very much appreciated, as it has brought the old diagrams back to life in a vibrant manner.

Jim Whiting of Capital Transport Publishing has been very supportive in getting this book into print; he had selected Justin Howes to design it but, tragically, Justin died when he had only just started work on the basic layout. He and I had only met once to discuss the detail. Richard Bates then took up the task and I am grateful to him for all the work he did to bring this book to reality.

Professional help has been received from Simon Murphy and Jonathan Riddell at London's Transport Museum in Covent Garden and at Acton, and particularly also from Beverley Cole and David Wright at the National Railway Museum in York. I am grateful to the Science and Society Picture Library (http://www.scienceandsociety.co.uk) for copyright permissions for one photograph in the NRM collection and for the British Railways maps which appear in Chapter 6. Tony Hargrave of Arriva Trains Northern kindly allowed reproduction of their map in Chapter 7.

I am also grateful to Andrew Grantham of *Railway Gazette International* for permission to reproduce items from past pages of that journal, including the one map by my father of which I do not have a copy.

My colleagues in Fastline Photographic Ltd, Steve Fountain and Seamus O'Neill, provided much needed assistance in photography and the reduction of that work to digital form. Their patience and dedication to getting good images from the originals is very much appreciated. I am grateful to Ruth Prosser for professional restoration work undertaken on some of my father's material, some of which may be unique, for illustration in this book. I received great encouragement and assistance from my good friend Richard Hall, who knows London's railways so much better than I, who went out on field research for me, and who accompanied me on some of my research forays to cast an eagle eye over all that we could find and see. We joked about his being my research assistant: many a true word was indeed spoken in jest.

Once again my wife Stephanie not only provided the support services so much needed by authors, but also was of material and valuable assistance in the production of this book.

I sense that this book may be incomplete, at least in Chapter One, where it appears that much research has yet to be done into the origins of the railway diagrammatic map. However the responsibility for errors, including those of omission, must rest with me and most certainly not with those who have been so helpful to me.

Contents

Introduction

From the early days, passengers needed help from the railway company.

Punch *cartoon c. 1902*

THE TWOPENNY TUBE

"Hi, guv'nor, there ain't no station named on this ticket!"
"No; all our tickets are alike."
"Then, 'ow do I know where I'm going?"

69

Although the use of diagrammatic devices within maps is probably as old as maps themselves, about a hundred years ago railwaymen started to look at the diagrammatic map with fresh eyes. Their involvement in transporting ever-increasing numbers of people on complex systems demanded that simple, rapidly understood and easily remembered information was presented to passengers on the move. Railway companies had long used map-makers who were understandably proud of the geographic fidelity and artistic attractions of their products, but the companies found that to keep passengers moving rapidly and in the right direction, a new approach was required. Part of this, of course, was the development of clear, unambiguous signage, but more was required than directions on the spot: the traveller needed to be able to plan ahead, and an evolution of the map was the way to do it.

The process took the form of the progressive simplification of the geographic map rather than a single act of invention: the diagrammatic map did not appear overnight. Now, many years later, we can see that the modern diagrammatic map, in its purest form, makes no reference to geographic features at all: the viewer can see where he is, and where he wishes to go, simply by reference to the lines, colours and symbols of the diagram, and without any prompting by the reality of geography. Many forms, styles and scales were tried in the first quarter of the twentieth century, and it was soon realised that symbols, properly used, could replace words: a new written language was indeed evolving. In that period the language was developed, codified, and refined. The process, it seems, was largely by trial and error, often undertaken by railwaymen rather than by the professional cartographers they employed for maps in timetables, carriage panels, and at stations.

The names of many of the artists – for that is what they were – now seem to be lost, but they produced a new means of communication specific to the needs of a railway system that, since 1897, was carrying over a billion passengers each year, and which had every incentive to handle such numbers with the greatest possible efficiency.

In the decade before the Second World War, the diagrammatic map became firmly established: accepted by hitherto sceptical managements, afraid that a new device might not work; and accepted by the public, who appreciated this new shorthand, devoid of flowery presentation, and in sympathy with contemporary design principles so well expressed in Art Deco and the streamline age.

Since the War, the diagrammatic map has survived, developed and succeeded. Any fear that it might be a fad has long since disappeared; it has been accepted all around the world as the only practical means of delivering directional information to people in a hurry and who need to be hurried along. Most of the development of this new language was undertaken in Great Britain by professional railwaymen, and their successors still rely upon the principles established when railways were only half as old as they are today.

1. Early diagrammatic railway maps

Railways do not get very far without maps. From the very moment of its conception, a railway needs maps to define its route, to attract capital, to seek legal authority, and to instruct surveyors, and then civil engineers. Once running, railways record their assets by reference to maps, they conduct maintenance, manage property, and settle disputes, all by reference to maps. The railwayman who has a good sense of railway geography is at a distinct advantage over one who has not.

Towards the end of the nineteenth century the railways of Great Britain realised the value of positive and attractive publicity. Timetables and posters were produced, increasingly in full colour as printing technology advanced, showing scenes near the railway as attractive destinations, and often accompanied by a map of the system. The maps were of small scale and very much simplified, with more or less straight lines which served to emphasize the directness of routes, and almost invariably they were supplied by commercial map-makers. The London & North Western Railway, for example, customarily showed its main line from Euston proceeding directly towards the Midlands, slightly west of north. It would not have done for such a map to show the truth, that in fact the line went west, and even south of west, before striking north, beyond Willesden.

And indeed, such detail was not necessary. It was more important that such a map, for such purposes, showed which towns and cities were connected with the system than any small detail of how they got there. In spite, therefore, of the minute detail of many railway maps, there were many special purposes for which only a minimum of information was required. In a simplified form, maps have thus long been used by railways to sell their services to customers, whether passenger, freight, or commercial advertising space. Timetables, whether as posters, brochures, leaflets, or in book form, are brought alive and made meaningful by maps. Not only can the company's own routes be shown, but places on other railways, served by means of running powers, show the full extent of the company's services[1]. But such maps can be ruthlessly biased: routes not used by the issuing company are either shown in very light lines, or omitted altogether.

Over the years, specialist forms of map have been developed. At the top of the tree, so to speak, is the highly detailed civil engineer's map, used to record every feature of a line that needed maintenance or which brought with it responsibility, such as occupation crossings, underline mine workings, watercourses of all kinds over and under the line, and structures. Below this, in lesser detail, has long been a great variety in number and type, prepared specifically for recording and illustrating particular information, very often to the exclusion of information irrelevant to the

1. It was once commonplace for timetable maps to show the full extent of through services, thereby creating the impression that the company's system was more extensive than it truly was.

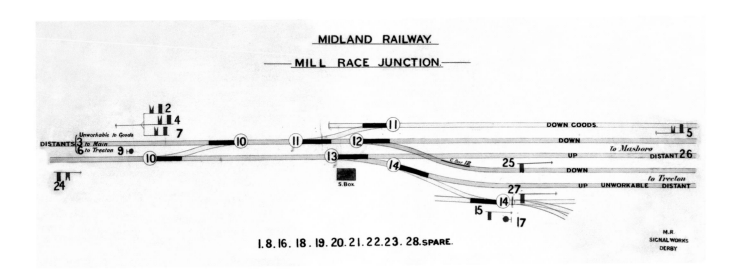

specialist user. Some of these maps were close to simple diagrams, and developed their own style of presenting information. One of the earliest, used strictly for internal purposes only, was the signal box diagram[2]. Whether it is best described as a simple diagram, or a map in diagrammatic form, is open to argument but signal box diagrams unquestionably have the features of a diagrammatic map [1.1].

We must be careful with our terminology here. The Oxford English Dictionary[3] defines a diagram as "that which is marked out by lines, a geometrical figure . . ." It states further, at 2., "An illustrative figure which, without representing the exact appearance of an object, gives an outline or general scheme, so as to exhibit that shape and relations of its various parts."

It does not interfere with those definitions if we develop an understanding of those words and say that the railway diagrammatic map has:

(a) lines;
(b) in geometrical form;
(c) which do not represent the exact appearance (of the line in question);
(d) but which exhibit the relations of its various parts;
(e) and which are supported by the barest necessary topographical information.

If this suggested understanding is accepted, then we can recognise a distinction between these essential characteristics and other features, which are more matters of style.

We need to question these thoughts a little. *Lines in geometrical form* is generally regarded these days as meaning straight lines. Very few modern diagrammatic maps have many curved lines, except short sections to designate railway junctions. But this can not mean that a diagram with extensively curved lines is not diagrammatic. And a map which is

1.1 A typical simple signal box diagram, from 1906. The junctions are shown compressed in length and simplified in layout. The fact that the main line is on a slight curve is ignored. Mill Race Junction was in Sheffield, 2m 36c north of the Midland Station.

Roy F Burrows Trust.

2. The oldest in the collection at National Railway Museum is from 1875, but the use of signal box diagrams is thought to predate this by several years - possibly by ten or more. Signal boxes, in which such diagrams were installed, dated from the 1860s.

3. Oxford English Dictionary, CD version, 1992.

comprised predominantly of straight lines set at half a dozen different angles is no less diagrammatic that one with few angles. All of these features, whether essential or of style, are designed to serve the purpose of giving accurate information very rapidly through ease of comprehension and speed of reading. The *geometrical form* must be allowed to mean that the lines (in other words, the railway lines) are laid out on the map purely to achieve a pattern or shape: this is the point at which departure from geographical accuracy takes place, and at which we can see that there is another form of map, referred to often in this book, called the *simplified geographical* map. In this, the lines remain more or less accurate geographically, but they incorporate the simplified symbology which is also one of the principal characteristics of the purely diagrammatic map.[4] In due course, that symbology included the enhanced disciplines of placing station names exclusively in horizontal lines, and preferably all on the same side of the line of route, simply to speed the process of reading the station names.

The signal box type of track diagram also appeared on system maps commonly prepared by the chief engineer's department of main line railways. These were pseudo-geographical, with the system laid out on more or less geographical lines and certainly respecting the points of the compass, but with local areas enlarged to show station layouts, yards and sidings. Examples which spring readily to mind are the magnificent Distance Book prepared by the Midland Railway, in which the entire system was shown in detailed maps on several score pages, and the folding maps prepared by the Great Eastern Railway and the Midland & Great Northern Joint Railway.

The rules being observed in these cases recognised that with area maps, the basic rule of north at the top has to be observed to give the viewer a sense of direction. In a signal box, the diagram may show east at the left if the box is facing south, so that the diagram is aligned in the same sense as the track outside. On single-line route maps, however, which were usually only used in passenger train vehicles, the line is simply displayed with a horizontal line, even if in fact the line in question runs north–south or in any one of a number of directions, and regardless of its curvature in doing so. It is not unknown for single-line route diagrams to be in handed pairs (showing the map either side of the car with the stations matching the order in which they appear outside), providing, of course that the carriages are never turned.

The Chief Engineer's or Civil Engineer's department was also responsible for the preparation of another special form of railway map, the gradient diagram, which railways have used from the earliest days and which is developed from levels taken by surveyors. This may not be thought of as a map, but as it traces the path of a railway in straight lines, from place to place, albeit in a vertical plane rather than horizontal,

4. A good example of this is the collection of junction maps issued by the Railway Clearing House, to designate ownership of the comprising lines; confusingly they were referred to as junction diagrams, but they were, nonetheless, geographical in their layout.

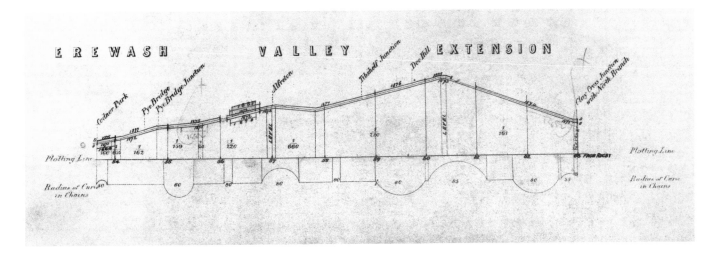

it must be regarded as such. And without question, it is diagrammatic, particularly in the vertical [1.2].

All of these clinically descriptive forms of map were in great contrast to the illustrated, and often complex and colourful posters which railways prepared to attract custom. The new technologies of colour printing were used by the railways in promoting the use of the railway system as it approached its zenith in the years immediately prior to the Great War. All sorts of technical developments, some of which had been around for years but which took time to be accepted and brought together, served to bring about faster, more comfortable and safer trains, and traffic was booming. In 1897, just over one thousand million passenger journeys were made on the main line railways of England, Scotland and Wales, this figure *excluding* those made by season ticket holders, who were some 1.1 million in number.[5]

Railway managers began to realise that passengers needed route information not only at stations but also while *en route*. This was generations before the introduction of public address systems. The commonest way to meet this need was to place a map of the system in each compartment or saloon. The display space most commonly available was on the compartment dividing wall, above a seat-back and below the luggage rack, but the shape of this space rarely met the needs of a map in a country that is, geographically, more north–south than east–west. Companies south and west of the Thames found this less of a problem, for their lines were short on the north–south axis, while the Great Western, which reached as far north as Birkenhead, found it necessary to compress the north–south scale of its maps. Many others simply showed their maps on a scale small enough for the area, no matter its shape, to be covered.

Either way, such maps were usually of the entire system of the company, because any carriage might serve anywhere on that system. This was a fact fundamental to the use of maps in carriages. Some companies, however, developed electrified lines which kept dedicated

1.2 The gradient diagram was well established for many years before other forms of diagrammatic railway map. This Midland Railway diagram dates from 1869, and shows not only the vertical characteristics of the line, with height exaggerated in relation to distance but without vertical transition curves. Also, below it, horizontal curvature is shown in purely diagrammatic form.

Roy F Burrows Trust.

5. If the season ticket holders each made five return journeys every week for fifty weeks of the year, they would between them contribute a further 550 million journeys to the total given, This calculation ignores the then common practice of working on Saturday mornings, but recognises that not all travelled every day.

1.3 Probably the first poster displayed in Great Britain to show a modern diagrammatic map was this design by H W Mesdag of Holland.

1.4 The earliest and simplest diagrammatic map found by the author was incorporated in a Great Central poster of 1904, advertising cheap fares on suburban lines in Manchester with a small coloured panel surrounded by letterpress. Unfortunately only this black and white photograph survives.

stock on a limited number of routes, and within these carriages very simplified route maps were displayed. In these we can see the origins of the truly diagrammatic map, where the colourful and decorated public map was supplanted by the simple factuality of the engineer's diagram.

Research suggests that although there were isolated examples of diagrammatic maps produced for posters and post cards from Edwardian days, the route diagram in carriages preceded the systematic development of diagrammatic maps on posters. Posters could be effective, but as the detail could only be seen at the station, it had to be memorised by the passing passenger if it was to be of use during the journey. That is why the poster gives only the simplest of messages, qualities to be associated with the company, and to be remembered by the passer-by for future reference: Speed; Directness; We can take you from here to Birmingham; or, No, we don't serve Great Yarmouth.

It is distinctly possible that the move towards modern diagrammatic presentation started with a Dutchman, Henrik Willem Mesdag (1831–1915), who specialised in marine paintings and who in 1900 produced a poster for the ferry service between Hook of Holland and Harwich [1.3]. This poster was displayed extensively on railway stations in Britain, and used unrefined but effective diagrams to represent the railways into the

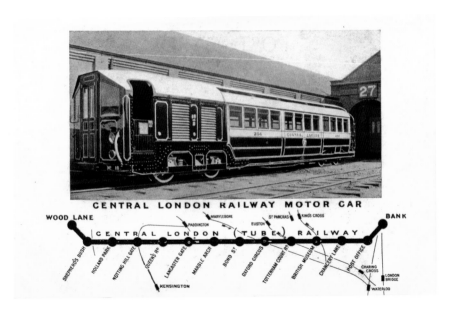

CENTRAL LONDON RAILWAY MOTOR CAR

1.5 This Central London Railway map, within a post card, is thought to date from 1904.

John Alsop collection

two ports.[6] His device for showing stations, an encircled solid disc, joined by thick straight lines, was imitated by the Great Central Railway in a poster of March 1904. Under the energetic and imaginative leadership of Sam Fay, this company introduced Weekly Zone tickets for suburban stations between Manchester London Road, Guide Bridge, and Fallowfield. The area of applicability was illustrated in the introductory poster by means of a simple diagrammatic map, with the background in two colours to designate two zones [1.4]. The line to Guide Bridge was shown almost straight (which in reality it was not), with the stations at equal distances, and the line down to Fallowfield in straight sections between stations. Stations on that line were spaced to allow other text to be placed between them. This map was small, simple, and effective.

At about this time, possibly in 1904 or a little later, the Central London Railway produced some post cards to publicise the line, which had opened in 1900 [1.5]. Designs included views of rolling stock and Lots Road power station, and incorporated a simple map of the line. With the exception of the extreme ends of the line, which for some reason were turned up at about 45 degrees, the line was shown straight, with stations equally spaced. It was not purely diagrammatic as we now understand that word, as can be seen from the illustration shown, but it was a sure step towards diagrammatic presentation. It is doubtful that the designs were used as posters, and no evidence has been found that they were used in trains.

The Bakerloo line, which opened as the Baker Street & Waterloo in 1906, used imaginative and eye-catching advertisements. One of the earliest showed the many connections with main line companies as a series of links, produced in 1907. It was by no means a diagrammatic map as we would now recognise it, but it was a real effort to break with the traditional map and to come up with a new method of presentation.

6. Reproduced from *Harwich and the Continent*, by Charles Wilson, published by the LNER, 1947.

15

1.6 Metropolitan and District map, of an unknown date. The search continues.

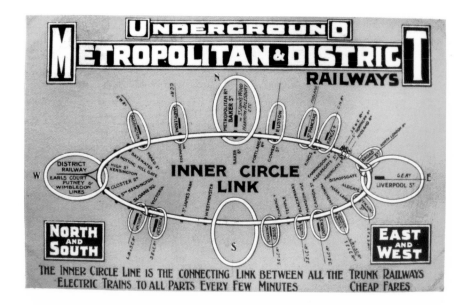

1.7 The Central London, having taken a lead with the purely diagrammatic representation of the route, stepped to the rear with this later map, showing streets and a meandering line.

1.8 Limited use was made of this complex and idiosyncratic design by the City & South London Railway, from a postcard.

Richard Casserley collection

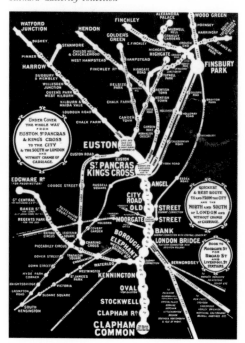

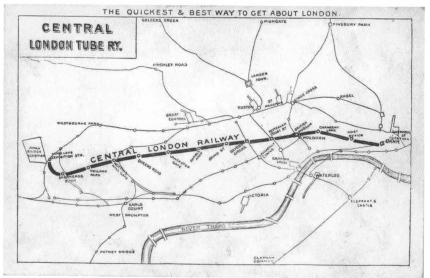

The idea of a railway forming a link with others was also exploited by the Metropolitan and District Railways, this time with an oval map, as represented by the Inner Circle, with links to other companies' lines [1.6]. The date of the accompanying poster is not known, but like the Bakerloo map, it is known to have been used as a post card in 1909. It is another example of an early search for something new: some way of simplifying the message was being keenly sought.

In 1908 the Central London produced another card, dedicated entirely to the map shown. It was a move away from the more diagrammatic map of 1904, but shows that the CLR was keen to develop means of simplifying the conventional geographical map, which typically at that time, was more geographical and was full of streets and other surface features [1.7].

Also in 1908, the City & South London Railway was using, for minor correspondence, a post card with the white-on-black map shown [1.8]. It is notable, not only for its complexity, but also for its curious mix of simplified geographical presentation for its own line, and diagrammatic presentation for others, including the L&NWR main line and the LB&SCR. The C&SL line is crudely shown, with a very thick line and gross solid circles for the stations, giving an impression of anything but a railway line upon which one could travel rapidly. Perhaps the artist was thus showing his preferences. It was clearly aimed at passengers to and from the north, telling them that there was no need to cross London on the surface if travelling to the City, or go to Waterloo or Victoria if further, to The Oval or Clapham. It is not known if this design was used for a poster, but certainly its eclectic style did not last.[7]

The Bakerloo was first shown in a recognisably diagrammatic form in a poster of 1908, albeit that the lines of the map are almost subordinate to the decorative panels showing attractions that could be reached by the Bakerloo.[8] But the diagrammatic elements of this map appear to have passed most map designers by [1.9].

In 1909 the London & North Western Railway produced a poster embodying a map of its routes from Liverpool and Manchester, through Birmingham and Willesden, to the south coast resorts of Brighton and Eastbourne, in connection with the *Sunny South Express* service that it ran with the London Brighton & South Coast Railway[9] [1.10]. The route was shown as a simple series of curved lines, thick for direct services and thin for connections, and not paying too much attention to geographical accuracy. The map was simply a device to say "Here is the service: it's direct and convenient".

The development of metropolitan railways, and with them the need for rapid and easy communication between companies and passengers, was of course taking place in other countries. Visits by railwaymen from Britain to observe what was happening in the United States were fashionable at this time, and the appointment of railwaymen from the United States and Canada to senior positions in British companies, though rare, was not unknown. Increasingly, too, trade publications from either side of the Atlantic crossed the ocean and were seen by senior managers more or less routinely.

In about 1910, the Los Angeles Pacific, to become a component of the Pacific Electric system (created by merger of several lines) in 1911, had produced a map that requires very careful descriptive language to exclude it from the layman's understanding of what a diagrammatic map is [1.11]. And in 1913 the suburban lines in Chicago, which included the famous L line around the Loop in the downtown area, produced a map which appears to be wholly diagrammatic [1.12]. However, this was only by default; it was in fact geographical, and the small deviations from straight lines were required as particular road junctions were followed. In addition

7. In Edwardian days the post card was very popular. Many railway companies reduced their posters to post card size, for their own use and for sale to the public. At this distance in time it is not always possible to know if many designs of post cards were originally prepared for posters, or for cards in their own right.

8. Mark Ovendon, *Metro maps of the world*, 2003, p.20.

9. To be seen in *The Railway Magazine* for November 1909, p.428.

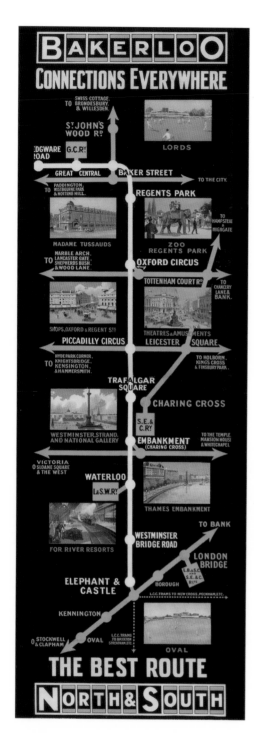

1.9 Baker Street & Waterloo poster of 1908, showing a very early use of simple diagrammatic presentation.

London's Transport Museum

1.10 Black and white LNWR poster for the *Sunny South Express* reproduced from *The Railway Magazine*, November 1909.

The Railway Magazine

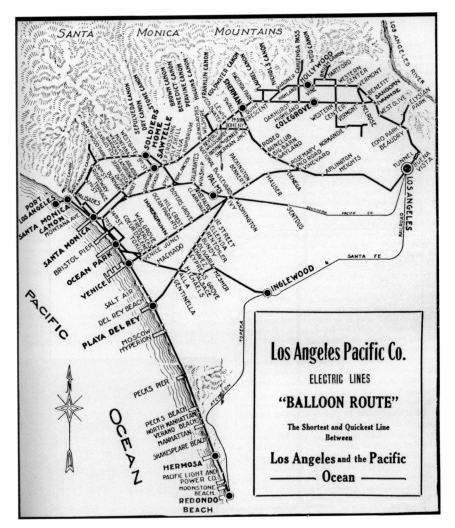

1.11 The Los Angeles Pacific was a predecessor company of the Pacific Electric system. This map dates from approximately 1911.

1.12 The Chicago elevated railway was built above streets and thus followed their grid pattern. This dates from 1913.

1.13 This diagram, within a 1911 letterpress poster of the GWR, was an early attempt to equate speed and directness through comparison with what the public thought flying achieved.

The Railway Magazine

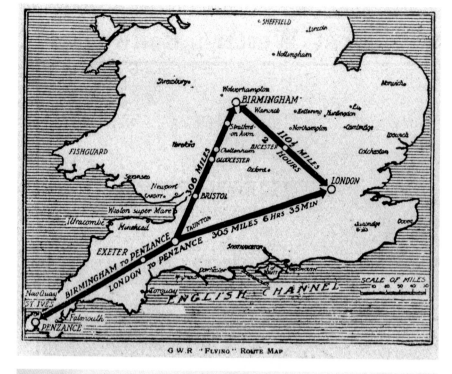

G.W.R. "FLYING" ROUTE MAP

1.14 *The Railway Magazine* March 1913 showed two slightly differing versions of this LNWR poster of electrified lines in London, of which this was the clearest.

The Railway Magazine

10. The first officially recognised powered flight in England was made in 1908 by S F Cody. The map was reproduced in *The Railway Magazine*, September 1911, p.260.

11. It was silent on the matter of early aeroplanes being easily blown off course and rarely following a straight line, and the fact that pioneer pilots navigated by the simple process of following railway lines as they meandered across the country!

12. Reproduced in *The Railway Magazine*, March 1913, pp.241 and 247

the fact that all adjacent streets were shown in the map, demands its classification as a geographical map. But there, thanks to the almost perfect grid pattern of the streets, was a map shouting out the benefits of diagrammatic presentation. Seemingly, no one noticed.

In 1911, the Great Western Railway produced a poster, mainly text, but including a small map, seeking to emphasise the speed of its services by reference to the new phenomenon of flying[10] [1.13]. Maps showing the exploits of early aviators often showed their conquests of the air by means of straight lines on the map, and in its poster the Great Western was keen to capitalise on this vogue of speed and directness, even though it was not yet a public form of transport.[11]

In early 1913, for example, the London & North Western Railway produced a poster map of its London suburban lines out of Broad Street and Euston[12] [1.14]. While not fully diagrammatic, it is aligned left–right rather than the north–south orientation which one associates with those lines, and is clearly an effort to recognise that something needed to be done

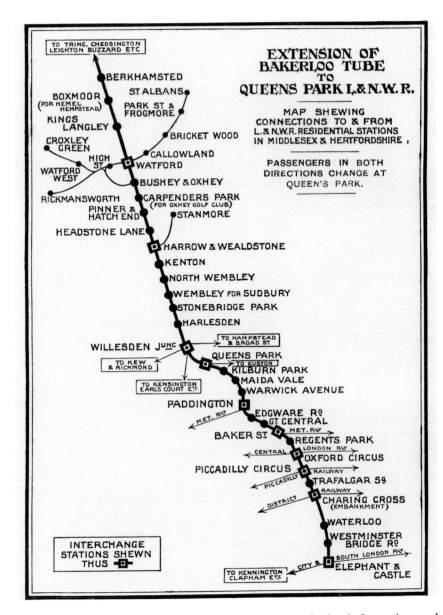

1.15 *The Railway Magazine* also published this map of LNWR and underground lines, to show connexions, in 1915.

The Railway Magazine

to rearrange the conventional map to address particular information and display requirements.

The Bakerloo had also featured in a map which appeared in *The Railway Magazine* in March 1915, which is a simplified geographical map, but which is interesting because it shows an early example of a distinction between ordinary stations (a solid circle) and interchange stations (open square and large dot within), but also because of its lack of discipline. To the unwary, not seeing a brief note of explanation, it suggests that one may travel, without changing, from Berkhamsted to Elephant & Castle [1.15]. It is not known whether this was drawn by the company or, more likely, by the publisher of the magazine.[13] But the fact of it may have prompted the Underground companies, a few years later, to

13. *The Railway Magazine* March 1915, p.255.

1.16 *The Railway Year Book*, 1917 included a map showing the theatre area of London's West End, all accessible by Underground.

Railway Year Book

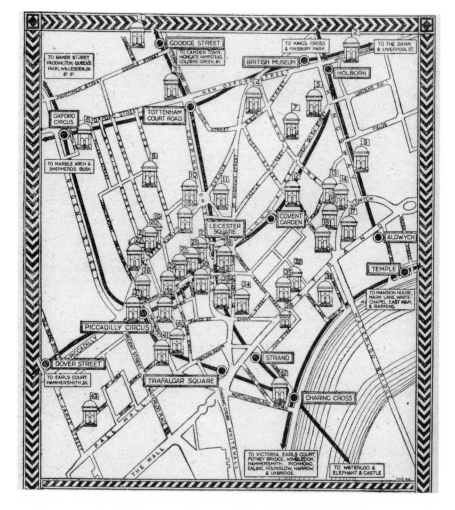

14. Mark Ovendon, *Metro maps of the world*, 2003, p.9.

15. The London system of underground railways was reorganised more than once over the years, and has appeared under several corporate names. For simplicity, the term *Underground* or *London Underground* has been used throughout this text even though it was not necessarily known by that name at the time in question.

16. All of this underlines the need for more detailed research into the origins of posters and other advertising material employed by the railways in the years prior to the First World War. The evolution of the diagrammatic map is but a part of this story.

produce a simplified geographical map of the London Underground system, which appeared in 1919.[14, 15] Meanwhile, another map showing attractions served by Underground railways serving London's "Theatreland" had appeared in the *Railway Year Book* in 1917. It used Mesdag's encircled solid discs for stations [1.16].

In all of these instances, and there were others, a simple message of directness and convenience was all that was to be said. They, together with signal box and gradient diagrams, have been mentioned to demonstrate that the railways themselves developed means of simple and direct pictorial illustration to deliver simple messages, in each case specialised to the use in question. There is little evidence that professional cartographers had a hand in any of these designs. The more pictorial examples probably came from illustrators employed to produce posters, and in some cases commissioned to incorporate maps in their designs. The simpler maps very probably came from draughtsmen employed by the companies, assisting whatever department was responsible for advertising the company's services.[16]

Some of these posters concerned long distance travel. There was also growing suburban traffic, on an increasing number of very busy lines, most of which ran into termini but which offered cross-town journeys through connecting stations. Suburban railways were now competing with the electric tram, and station stops were brief. Here was an entirely different problem of passenger communication. Passengers needed to be able to confirm, *en route*, that they were going in the right direction, had correctly remembered the station at which they had to change trains, and that they had only so many stops to go before alighting. This preparation had to be made to ensure quick stops, for the railway company, as well as the passenger, benefited from the passenger being ready to alight and being sure of which way to go when he had. Passengers who interrupted the flow of people through a station caused delay and cost time. In the circumstances of a crowded train and short distances between quick stops (particularly as achieved on the electric services) a form of map was required that concentrated solely on giving this accurate information, and no more, very quickly. The single-line route map had made a start in this process, but many railways operated stock over more than one suburban route, and sold tickets for destinations all over their systems. A different approach to passenger information was required.

Here in the early years of the twenty-first century we take the suburban railway map for granted. In the large cities it is ubiquitous. In London it is famous, and the London Underground map is regarded by some as an icon. It appears on stations, in pocket diaries, and on post cards and tea-towels. It is instantly recognisable. But it was not, as has been claimed, "invented".

Although London Underground had long had a reputation for the excellence of the way in which it guided the unfamiliar passenger to the correct platform and on to the correct train, for many years it concentrated on publishing strictly geographical maps of its system. It was not alone in having the problem of telling passengers, quickly and directly, how to get from here to there: all the main line companies with substantial suburban services had the same problem.

The first application of nascent diagrammatic map techniques to route maps in main line passenger carriages appears not to have been recorded as such, but included in the collection of photographs at National Railway Museum are several interior views of Lancashire & Yorkshire Railway electric stock built for the electrification of the line between Liverpool and Southport. The earliest of these appears to have been taken in 1910, when some new stock was built. Within, across the cars on a bulkhead over a door, was a distinctive map which is well on the way to being diagrammatic [1.17]. The north–south line is shown horizontally, and the layout is simplified geographically. It shows the electrification to have gone only as far as Maghull on the Ormskirk line,

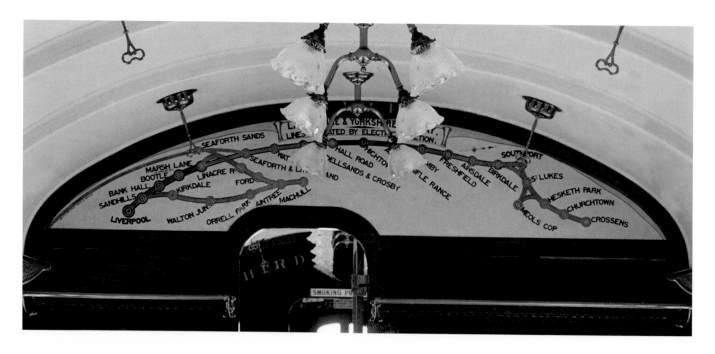

1.17 An L&YR car typical of the electrified stock used on the Liverpool-Southport line, contained the earliest known dedicated route map.

NRM: HOR F791

while other views of L&Y electric stock show the line all the way to Ormskirk. Other photographs taken at the same time showed that the map had to be drawn several times, identical in its information, but slightly differing in shape according to the bulkhead on which it was to be displayed. There was a lot of effort needed here, but clearly the L&Y thought it was worth it.

The service between Liverpool and Southport had been electrified in 1904, and the map was probably produced for the opening. Interior photographs of the original rolling stock are insufficiently clear to show if maps were used in 1904. Certainly in 1910 no distinction was made between ordinary and interchange stations. As it was turned through ninety degrees and the stations placed at equal spacings, the layout could not be much further removed from geographical, and although it does not bear the straight lines that we expect of diagrammatic maps today, it is clearly a map in diagrammatic form, and an important step in the evolution of the modern diagrammatic map. In particular it shows that this kind of map did not originate in a need to get away from the cluttering of streets and other surface detail, but rather that it needed to show a simple sequence of stations quite apart from any other distractions. In this the stations are shown at equal distance from each other. This selective compression gave the appearance of equal importance to all of the stations, and allowed station names to be prominent without being squeezed together or allowing waste empty spaces between them. It is a remarkable exercise of economy of space. The colours, artist, and date of execution are not known. The same is true of a simplified geographical map used in the cars of the L&Y electrified services from Bury to Holcombe Brook, which

line used overhead wires rather than the third rail of the service from Manchester to Bury, which was electrified in 1916.

The L&Y was probably alone in the use of a special map for short distance services at this time. No evidence has been found of such maps where one might expect to find them, whether diagrammatic or geographical. The tiny Volk's Electric Railway at Brighton, Britain's first, had open sided cars and thus nowhere to place a map. The Liverpool Overhead Railway, the Mersey Railway, the North Eastern Tyneside electrification, the Midland Railway's electrification between Morecambe and Heysham, and the LNWR's electrification of suburban lines from Euston in 1914 all appeared to be without special maps. The pioneers of electrification south of the Thames, the London Brighton & South Coast and London & South Western Railways seem not to have produced special maps or to have used diagrammatic techniques at this time, although the Brighton did issue the card shown [1.18], this example dating from 1911, playing with the idea of new presentation but not going as far as formal diagrammatic design.

It was in about 1908, or perhaps as late as 1910, that the District Railway produced a route diagram for use in its trains [1.19, 1.20]. This map, probably the earliest purely diagrammatic route diagram found thus far, shows the entire line from Ealing Broadway to Barking as a straight line, with nine branches off. The stations are not quite equidistant, although the effect is that they are, and all station names are shown in sans-serif letters. Interchange stations are shown with their names in red;

1.20 Detail of the 1908 District Line map to show the rendering of interchange stations in red, and the condensed typeface.

London's Transport Museum

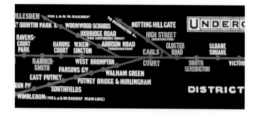

1.19 The District Line used this purely diagrammatic map from about 1908. It is the earliest purely diagrammatic route diagram found so far.

London's Transport Museum

1.21 Johnston's new typeface was applied to this Piccadilly route diagram in 1916 but it is not certain that it was used in trains.

London's Transport Museum

points at which to change for the branches are not highlighted this way, and the lines with which interchange may be made are not shown.

This style of route map does not seem to have survived to be used on other railways. The basic idea is exactly what was later realised was necessary; perhaps its presentation, reversed out of black, restricted its popularity. It was, in any case, regarded as difficult to print, and the surviving example shows less than prefect registration of the colours used for the station names.

In 1916 another attempt to use the diagrammatic route map, possibly in trains, was made, this time for the Piccadilly, and using the then new Johnston lettering which had come into use that year. It was much more in line with what was to become so familiar [1.21]. Again it uses the basic horizontal straight line, with all stations shown as rings, and interchanges only designated by flags showing the routes available. The prominent directional arrows were not perpetuated in later maps.

Soon after the end of the Great War, the Underground group of companies entered this field in a more structured manner. Examination of photographs of carriage interiors, held in the collections at the London's Transport Museum, shows the use of diagrammatic route maps in the early 1920s on the District, Hampstead, Metropolitan, and City & South London Railways. Those of the first two were of strikingly similar style, using the Edward Johnston lettering introduced in 1916, and strictly diagrammatic. Indeed, in the case of the District Railway, the title on the map can be read as *District Railway Route Diagram* [1.22]. A re-creation of this map has been specially prepared for this book [1.23].

These maps continued the process of the development of a new language, a shorthand, or a code, which, once understood, gave messages

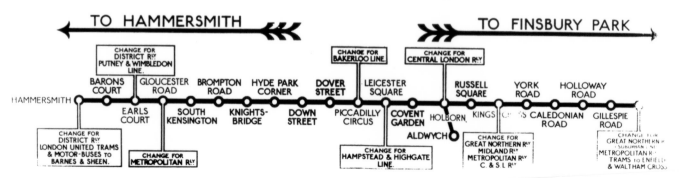

1.22 More complex was the District Railway route diagram recorded in about 1920, in London Underground photograph U267.

London's Transport Museum

1.23 Max Roberts has recreated the District route diagram for the author. It appeared in several forms as the line was extended: this is generated from the oblique view in the 1920 photograph.

Max Roberts

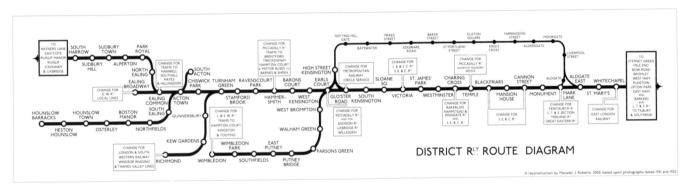

DISTRICT RLY ROUTE DIAGRAM

A reconstruction by Maxwell J. Roberts, 2005, based upon photographs dated 1921 and 1922

to passengers very quickly and efficiently. An earlier photograph is of the interior of Hampstead Line gate stock, taken in 1920, showing a map of very nearly the simplest kind, a thick horizontal line, although in reality the line was predominantly north–south [1.24]. At the right hand end of the map, the north end of the line has a fork, with lines off, at that time, to Highgate and Golders Green. At the other, left (south) end is shown a loop, at Charing Cross.[17] Interestingly, the map is also displayed along the car, on both sides over the windows, with north at the *left* end of the map, while its display across the car has north at the *right* end. If nothing else this ambidexterity of display required a mental agility among passengers when trying to remember the sequence of stations.[18] This was a particular problem for the Underground companies: as most of their lines were in tunnel, passengers had no view from the window to prompt their anticipation of their destination other than the brightly-lit stations. Knowing the sequence of stations was thus all the more important.[19] A re-creation of this map has also been prepared [1.25].

17. Developments of this map may be seen in photographs taken of car interiors in 1924 (87022) and 1928 (U5013). As the Hampstead line developed, so did the shape of the lines on the route diagram, and passengers had to become familiar with a succession of map layouts.

18. Included among them was Henry Beck, of whom more anon. He worked for London Underground and produced its first network diagrammatic map in 1932; it was published in January 1933. In his travel to work from Highgate to St James's Park, he can hardly have missed seeing this early example of a diagrammatic map, and that of the District Line, day in, day out.

19. Before the days of public address systems on trains, it was not unknown for seasoned travellers to rise from their seats without once looking out of the window, prompted by the familiar sound of a pair of points, a tunnel, or a particular lurch in the track. For the passenger less familiar with the route, abundant station signs and announcements from guards were necessary.

27

1.24 One of the earliest known route diagrams on the Underground appeared in Hampstead stock in about 1920. Here is such a diagram, seen in London Underground photograph U1047.

London's Transport Museum

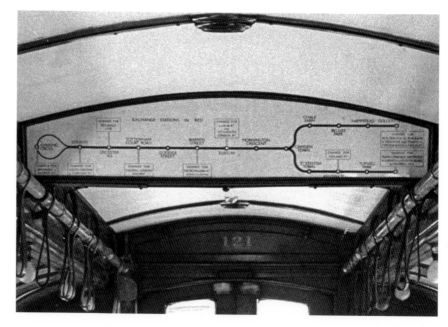

1.25 In the absence of an original route diagram, Max Roberts has specially recreated the 1920 Hampstead map to show its essential features.

Max Roberts

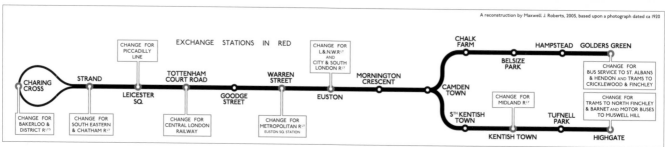

20. This was important because as the eye scans along the list of stations, the prominence of the station, breaking the even line of the route, tells the viewer to look for the name of the station. There is a slight danger that the single sided tick, which was used as a station indicator in the 1933 map, will allow the viewer to miss a station as the eye scans quickly, simply because both the tick and the name are on one side of the line and there is nothing to catch his eye on the other.

21. The designation of stations with the tick used by H. C. Beck in 1933 seems not to have migrated to route maps in carriages until well after the war. Standardisation of symbology and presentation between cars and posters on stations was undertaken by Tim Demuth in the 1970s, but even then this effort did not include track plates the enamel route diagrams opposite platform entrances. They, and all signage came under the Chief Electrical Engineer.

22. *The Railway Magazine*, February 1921, p.117, within an article about new passenger rolling stock. There are three different examples in the LT collection at Acton, one pre-grouping (shown here) and two from the 1920s.

The maps of 1920 have all the station names displayed horizontally, although they appear on alternate sides of the line of route. Their placement on a horizontal line helped to generate space for their display in a legible size of lettering. This pattern was soon well-established on London Underground diagrams, but at that time these diagrams also used a circle, (solid or open) to designate stations.[20]

This and other route diagrams on Underground cars in the 1920s show a lack of a single controlling mind on the smaller details of their design. The 1920 Hampstead diagram shows all stations as rings, whether or not they are interchanges. District Railway maps in 1920 show all stations as rings, but in 1927 distinguished between them while not using flags for details of the lines available for interchange; in the early 1930s they used diamonds for interchanges. The diagram in Piccadilly cars in the early 1920s used both solid circles and open rings without distinction regardless of whether they were exchange stations; this was corrected in about 1930, and in the streamlined cars of 1936 diagrams used solid circles exclusively. Bakerloo maps in the late 1930s showed all stations as rings.[21]

The Metropolitan map has been found in a photograph in 1921.[22] [1.26].

28

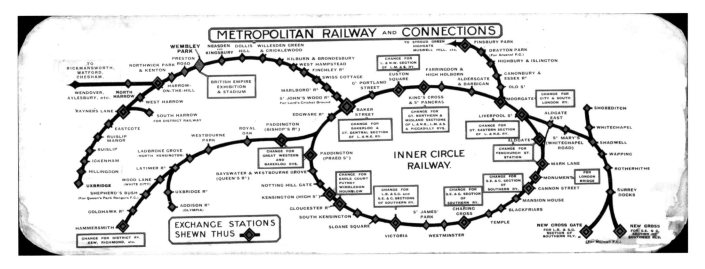

1.26 In 1921 the Metropolitan Railway produced this striking route diagram for use in their cars.

London's Transport Museum

1.27 The City & South London map, of unknown date, one of the few original route diagrams in the LU collection, sadly the worse for wear.

London's Transport Museum

It is characterised by its exclusive use of curved lines, with the "Inner Circle Railway" as an oval[23] with curved branches flying off at various places. It uses the diamond to indicate stations, and a larger diamond, and a smaller within, denotes interchange stations. It is undoubtedly not geographical, and it is unquestionably diagrammatic. A route map from a carriage, held in a private collection, shows the Metropolitan beyond Rickmansworth, going as far as Verney Junction, with the Brill branch still open, and thus dating the map before 1935. The use of Johnston lettering tells us that it was a Met. Railway map,[24] after July 1933, even though it is anonymous. It is all in black on a white card.

Of the first four maps mentioned above, that of the City & South London, photographed in 1922,[25] is the simplest, for it is but a straight line, albeit not using the Johnston lettering. That of the District, in 1921,[26] is the most complex, for that was then the nature of the District. It is a long line, with many branches. Unfortunately a copy of this early route diagram seems not to have survived to enter the Museum collection.

The LT collection contains very few original diagrammatic maps from carriages, but one of them is a City & South London route diagram [**1.27**]. It dates from 1922 or earlier, because connection references are to pre-Grouping main line companies. It probably replaced the version mentioned in the preceding paragraph. The line then ran from Clapham Common (shown at the left) to Euston. The use of Johnston lettering dates it after 1916. All stations are shown by a ring: no distinction is shown between interchanges and others. It is the route diagram in its simplest form.

23. Similar to the oval device used in the Met & District map mentioned earlier. It was to be used again, by George Dow in 1941 (see illustration in chapter 5), and by H. C. Beck in 1964.

24. Because the Underground had the sole right to use Johnston; the LNER used Gill Sans.

25. LTM ref 1999/9752.

26. LTM ref 1999/6815

2. The LNER and its Dowagrams, 1929–1931

2.1 George Dow at about the time that he drew the LNER's first two diagrammatic route maps, 1929.

2.2 The GE lines diagrammatic route map was the more complex of the two drawn by George Dow in 1929.

If increasing numbers of passengers were to be directed accurately and swiftly, not only through stations and on to trains, but also off them at the right stations, a fresh development in the presentation of route information was necessary. The chosen device had become the diagrammatic map, because by such a device, direct and immediate, all irrelevant information commonly included in a map – the reality of geography – could be ignored. The all-purpose all-informing conventional map available from map-making companies could be replaced by the single-purpose diagram, specially drawn by, or for, the using company. Such a device had many attractions, and indeed one of its offerings, the illusion of the journey being in a straight line, encouraged custom through its apparent efficiency. The twists and turns of the railway were not important to the passenger, who wanted to know where he was in relation to his station: How many stops is it before I get off? Where do I change trains? What is my route after I do? The diagrammatic map had evolved from techniques developed for simplified maps and diagrams, and long in existence. The next step in its evolution was taken by the London & North Eastern Railway.

The LNER had three London-based suburban systems, each one more extensive than any one of the Underground lines, reaching out from its termini at King's Cross, Fenchurch Street and Liverpool Street, and Marylebone. In the 1920s the routes from these stations were still known by their pre-Grouping names of Great Northern, Great Eastern and Great

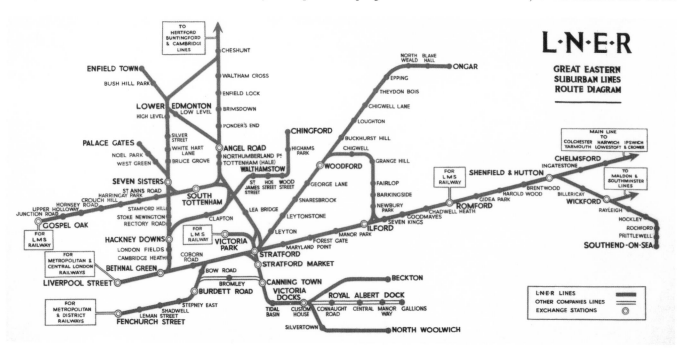

Central lines. The Great Northern Railway had started to introduce rolling stock in articulated sets (in fours) from 1920, and after the Grouping, the LNER introduced articulated sets (in fives) to the Great Eastern lines. All were steam-hauled, and it was therefore possible, if not likely, that any of the sets could have been moved away to service elsewhere on the LNER system.

It is not known what maps, if any, were placed in suburban stock compartments in early LNER days. Some Great Eastern stock had been equipped with an attractive coloured carriage panel which showed suburban lines in one quarter of the panel, alongside maps of the whole GER system and a small map of the Norfolk Broads. Whether or not this attractive trio of maps was placed in suburban stock is not known, but certainly it was not placed in the articulated sets built by the LNER. What maps may have been displayed in ex-GN stock is not known. It is possible that there were no maps at all, or that they were of the entire GN system.

Ordinarily the possibility of suburban stock being moved elsewhere on the LNER might have discouraged the use of a route map in these carriages, dedicated to particular routes, but in 1929 George Dow [2.1], then a member of the staff in the Chief General Manager's office at King's Cross, working in his own time and at his own initiative, designed and drew diagrammatic maps for the GE and GN lines [2.2 and 2.3]. They were designed specifically to be placed in compartments of passenger stock, and they were therefore sized and proportioned to fit in the standard glazed frames above seatbacks, with the lettering of a size readable from any corner of the compartment.

2.3 George Dow's GN lines route diagram, 1929.

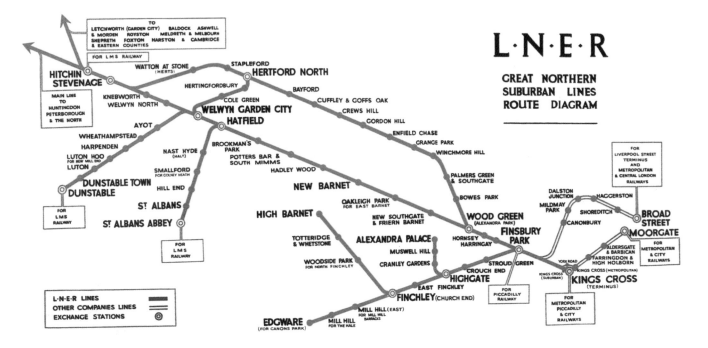

It is believed that these were the first diagrammatic maps ever designed for a whole system, termini, connections and branches included, as distinct from a single line of route. The significance of the difference is not only the extent but also the complexity, with exchange stations, and lines covering a large area rather than a single linear route. Potentially, therefore, the passenger's entire journey was shown, even if he had to change trains. With more than one major route depicted, such maps had to be very carefully laid out to give a sensible shape and a sense of direction for the traveller. In short, the need for clarity of presentation with such a volume of information was paramount if the purpose of such a map was not to be lost.

And there was a further significance. Although the Underground railways in London had been shown together in posters and other maps since 1908, in route diagrams within trains only the line of the company in question had been portrayed, and in general practice this was from a rather later date. It was to be many years before maps of the central London area, where the majority of the interchanges were to be found, were shown in trains. It is doubted that the entire London Underground system has ever been depicted in maps in trains.

The LNER maps showed the full suburban system from each of the main termini. That from Marylebone was physically separate from the King's Cross and Liverpool Street lines, and these two were only connected by the Tottenham & Hampstead joint line in the south and at Cambridge in the north. In other words, the LNER maps showed full suburban systems while the Underground route diagrams only showed the route being travelled, and if a connection was made on the Underground, the passenger had to research his route afresh in the second train.[1]

At the time George Dow was a grade five clerk of the age of 21. He had studied engineering drawing when he had been hoping to become a locomotive engineer and before family misfortune had prevented this. He had joined the LNER at King's Cross on 28 March 1927, and had been allocated to the Works Section of the Chief General Manager's office at King's Cross. There he had become involved in preparing maps and diagrams for internal purposes, usually schemes designed to save money or to improve service. A file of these maps still exists,[2] and shows that although most of them were strictly geographical, they were simple – stripped of all unnecessary information to allow the essential points to be made in the scheme to which they applied.

Accustomed to presenting the management with the bare, uncluttered information required, George Dow applied the same principle to his initiative in preparing route diagrams. He reckoned that the LNER needed to show simple maps in suburban compartments to ensure that passengers had ready information while *en route*.[3] In other words, he did not choose to produce a diagram suitable for a poster or a pocket folder, but instead

1. This was inevitable while Underground trains remained on one route all of their lives.

2. In the author's collection.

3. The LNER used compartment stock extensively for suburban traffic; the multiplicity of doors on the carriages allowed very smart station stops, so that passengers could alight and board very quickly.

chose to provide the information constantly while the passenger was travelling, and available at a glance.

Many years later he recorded that he had been impressed by the way in which the Underground companies kept their passengers informed. At the time George Dow designed the maps he was living at the family home in Matheson Road, Kensington, and he travelled to King's Cross by means of the District Railway from West Kensington, changing at Earl's Court to the Piccadilly to take him to King's Cross. At that time the Piccadilly's route map was very simple, but that of the District was somewhat more complex, and sitting within sight of it six days a week undoubtedly inspired George Dow to think of applying its principles to the needs of the LNER.

The common form of LNER main line suburban stock in those days had compartments. To be displayed in such carriages, the maps had to be placed on compartment walls above the seatbacks. The available picture frames, commonly used for pictorial matter, were landscape in format, and this demanded a treatment that ignored the realities of geography while retaining enough natural orientation for the passenger to retain his sense of direction. For this the diagrammatic map was particularly suited, as its form raised no expectations of geographical fidelity.

The choice of the diagrammatic form may have been easy – even startlingly obvious. But there was a problem of the density of information to be put in the space available. The most complex route diagram at that time was that of the District Railway. This comprised a main line of forty-eight stations and six branches serving another sixteen: a total of sixty-four. The route diagram partly visible in a 1927 photograph shows that not all of these appeared on the line of the diagram. The east end very probably was shown only as far as Whitechapel, and all sixteen stations east of there were shown in a flag. Certainly at least ten were so treated. The reason for this was a combination of the space available for the map, and the spacing of the stations selected by the artist. He had to recognise that the map had to be legible to passengers seated on the opposite side of the carriage, and probably by those standing at a greater distance. At the time Underground geographical poster maps commonly curtailed the District line somewhere in the area of Whitechapel, and flagged the stations to Southend. And so to adopt the same approach on diagrammatic route maps was seen as an acceptable practice.

In laying out the GE Lines map, for example, George Dow had a slightly different set of considerations. The GE line from Fenchurch Street to Southend served only twenty-six stations. The furthest that a passenger might be seated from the map would be a corner of a compartment – probably a little closer than a standing passenger in a District car. But George Dow did not only have to deal with the simplicity of a main line with a few relatively short branches: the GE lines comprised a further seventy-five stations on a maze of tracks incorporating twenty-one junctions.

The key to clear layout was to be found, at least in part, in the selection of line thickness, the relative size of stations, and their names. George Dow eschewed the idea of putting any suburban stations in a flag,[4] and chose a modest station size: each solid circle had a diameter of 1.6 times the line thickness. Each ring (interchange station) was about 2.25 times the line thickness. The interchanges did not seem oppressively large simply because they were open, not solid. It is fairly certain that he did not have to experiment with these proportions: the simplified geographical maps which he had been sketching for LNER senior management as part of his daily work typically showed larger circles for stations, and all on maps which were less intense and where space was not at such a premium. When he came to designing the intense GE and GN diagrammatic maps, the need for smaller station indication was obvious.[5]

He must have started by measuring the available spaces in the picture frames, for the maps which he drew were proportioned and sized for them. He laid out the GE lines, which run east and north from Liverpool Street and Fenchurch Street, rising from bottom left to top right. The GN lines, which run more or less due North from Kings Cross and Moorgate, were arranged to rise from bottom right to top left. This device imparted a sense of direction to the reader, but it also assisted the map-maker, for it created space for station names which was not so available on a horizontal line. On the GE lines map, the predominant angle for the lines is taken by the main line from Liverpool Street to Shenfield and beyond, paralleled by the line from Fenchurch Street below and the line from Gospel Oak to South Tottenham above. A similar device of parallel lines appears on the GN lines map, where the Hertford Loop is shown parallel to the main line through Welwyn.

It was in these features that George Dow grasped the essential difference, the necessary forward leap, in moving from the single-line route diagram to the system diagram. It was not enough to leave stations where they were, so to speak, and join them with straight lines, with each line between stations at a different angle from those on either side. Neither was it enough to have whole routes in straight lines, as on the route diagrams produced hitherto. Stations had to be moved not only in relation to the straight line on which they appeared, but also in relation to other lines nearby. All of the routes on a diagrammatic map – and here is the essential challenge of a system map – have to be arranged into a coherent form that is logical, memorable, and imparted a sense of direction to the user.

There were, on the 1929 LNER diagrams, two essential features that brought this coherence into being. One was the extensive use of parallel lines, whether on both sides of a loop, as on the GN Lines map, or of unconnected lines, as on the GE Lines map.[6] It is important,

4. But the continuation of the main lines to distant points were so indicated.

5. This process of coming to terms with the needs of an intense map was to confront H. C. Beck in due course. As can be seen from the early versions of his London Underground map, H. C. Beck at first tried to use solid circles for stations, and large ones at that. His had a diameter about 3.75 times line thickness, not the more modest 1.6 used by George Dow. But although the circle (solid or open) was standard practice on Underground route diagrams in trains, Beck did not retain them at a reduced diameter: instead he adopted the tick on one side of the line, the same height as line thickness.

6. The GE lines map would have had more parallel lines had it been possible to show the line to Chingford straight, and parallel with the line through Woodford. The need to avoid using the name *Walthamstow* three times, on each of the stations there, prevented this.

34

cartographically, that these lines were parallel, because this established the principle of what we might call lines of common angle. In the simplified geographical map, lines were set at angles which simulated the true geographical map; in the simple route diagram, a single horizontal line ignored geography entirely. But in the diagrammatic system map, rather than having many lines at as many different angles, the placement of several lines at the same angle (either parallel or mirrored either side of the vertical or horizontal) gave the map a shape and a new discipline. George Dow did not use lines of common angle exclusively on these two maps, but he made a significant step in that direction. Secondly, then, there is, in the disposition of lines below Finsbury Park in the GN Lines map, a tentative first use of common angles either side of the vertical. On this map, the line to Edgware is only a degree or so off being at a common angle (off the horizontal) with the East Coast Main Line through New Barnet. To many observers, perhaps, it appears to be at a common angle. The device also appears, just, on the GE Lines map with the lines passing through Burdett Road and Canning Town.

This device had never been necessary on most of the route diagrams produced hitherto, for they had rarely contained enough lines for this to be needed. It will have been seen that the Hampstead and District route diagrams of 1920 and 1921 both featured parallel *horizontal* lines, but George Dow's GE lines map was the first to have parallel lines at angles other than the horizontal. It was also the first to make significant use of vertical lines.

The straight lines delivered clarity, but also a second message: "this is a direct route, unlike buses and trams." Stations were simple solid circles ("here you may alight"); or rings ("here you may change trains")[7]; stations were shown equidistant ("your journey is not as far as you thought"); all stations bore their names on the same side of the line ("here is a simple list from which to read"). This latter device had been used almost exclusively on the curvaceous Metropolitan map of 1921, while all of the subsequent Underground route maps had the station names placed on alternate sides of the line, presumably to generate space for larger lettering. On the GE Lines map, the names appear on the same side of the line even where it is horizontal, where hitherto designers had placed names on alternate sides simply to generate space for the lettering. The use of the horizontal line can easily create this problem.

Another cartographic device introduced to the diagrammatic map with both the GN and GE Lines maps was the pair of thin lines – a double line known to cartographers as casing – to designate connecting routes of other companies. The light line inside the casing reduced the visual weight and therefore perceived importance of such lines. These were shown whether or not the LNER had running powers over those lines. George Dow did this extensively on the on the GN map, showing the Metropolitan line to

7. An open ring had been used to designate an interchange station on a Metropolitan Railway pocket map in 1924.

35

Moorgate and the LMS to Broad Street.[8] Their use on the GE map was less extensive, having to show only the use of the LMS through Bromley and the Port of London Authority line to Gallions.

Here in all these characteristics was a simple language, effectively and attractively arranged, arguably in a slightly more finished manner in the GE Lines map.

The maps were undoubtedly complex: The GN suburban lines map incorporated eleven junctions and 71 stations, while that for the GE lines showed 21 junctions and 101 stations. The cartographic demands of laying out such a number of lines, flying off in all directions, while leaving enough room for clear display of station names, can not be exaggerated.

The principal requirement was that the maps, although they were diagrammatic, had to have a recognisable shape. Little use would be served by a map that had the traveller searching fruitlessly for where he had started his journey. The termini and interchange stations were given names in larger lettering. Both maps showed stations at equidistant separations regardless of how far apart they were on the ground. The interchange stations shown were not only for connections within the LNER; other companies' lines were also highlighted.

The LNER was delighted with George Dow's initiative. W M Teasdale, to whom he offered them, not only took the maps for reproduction and placement in suburban trains, but he also decided that the quality of the draughtsmanship was so good that setting them up in type was not necessary. The maps were put into use that year, and were illustrated in the *Railway Gazette* and in the LNER company magazine in June 1929. The maps were printed with red lines and black lettering on white card, and were placed in hundreds of suburban carriages on the GE and GN routes. They were received enthusiastically by the technical press: the *Railway Gazette* later recorded that George Dow's maps had collectively been dubbed "Dowagrams", although it did not say who coined this expression.[9]

It is significant that the maps were drawn for display in carriages: the passenger no longer had to remember what he had seen on a map in the station or what he had been told in the booking office. But because of the shape and limitations of the available space above compartment seatbacks, lines had to go across the map whilst established mapping conventions would have most of them arranged up and down the map.[10] With hindsight we can see that the maps might have had more style had they incorporated fewer different angles for the various branch lines. The 1933 Beck map of London Underground lines, with its concentration on 90 and 45 degrees, unquestionably set a fashion in this respect which has endured to this day. But the enforced shape of the 1929 maps influenced their layout, and it is interesting to note that none of the early Underground route diagrams, all of which were also displayed in trains where little

8. F H Stingemore had shown the Finsbury Park to Moorgate line as casing, on his geographical maps of 1926 and 1931. Earlier it had been shown on Underground maps as a solid, then as hatched, line. Other maps at this time showed it as solid, in Metropolitan purple, and therefore undistinguished from other Met. lines. The LNER continued to work the services, although the line had been owned by the Met. since 1913.

9. *Railway Gazette* 1 October 1937.

10. This was particularly true of the LNER's GN lines which proceeded more or less due north from King's Cross.

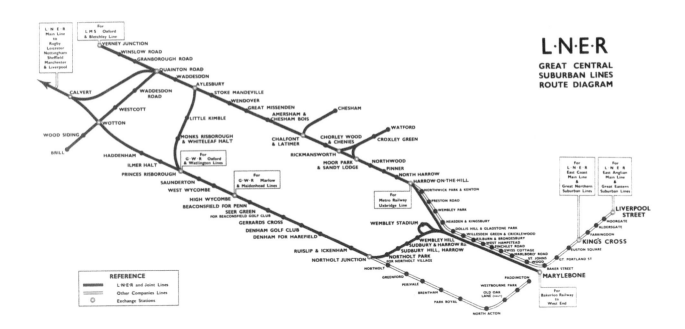

vertical space was available, were able to use the freer style which H. C. Beck was able to exploit on his pocket maps and posters.

In 1929 the LNER amended its rules for cheap day tickets. Brochures were published for both the GN and GE lines, and although they shared the same passenger manager, the maps used to show the applicability for the cheap fares were markedly different in style. That for the GN lines was geographical, attractively sinuous and slightly informal, showing lines from King's Cross (but not Moorgate) to Dunstable Town and Royston. That for GE lines was diagrammatic, with the appearance of asymmetric candelabra. It was a little indisciplined, by the standards of other diagrammatic maps,[11] but it was distinguished, in a minor way, for its re-introduction of the internal tick to designate stations. This had been used by the Great Northern Railway on geographical maps some years before. The brochures which survive are dated June 1929, which indicates that the new fares were introduced with the Summer timetable. As far as is known, George Dow was not involved with either map.

In 1932 a further map [2.4], designed on all the same principles as the GN and GE maps, was produced by George Dow at the request of the LNER, for the suburban carriages working on the Great Central lines from Marylebone. It also showed lines from Paddington and Liverpool Street, once again using his device of casing to indicate connecting service over other companies' lines.[12] The same hallmark of lines of common angle is to be seen dominating the map, as well as the determination to place station names on the same side of the line wherever possible.

By this time, the LNER had firmly committed itself to the widespread use of Gill Sans typeface, and George Dow's design was in this instance

2.4 In 1932 the LNER introduced George Dow's diagrammatic route map to the GC lines, but typeset it in Gill Sans.

11. For example, it did not differentiate interchange stations and some station names were shown off the horizontal. But it was not intended as a travel map, rather as an illustrated list of stations.

12. The inclusion of the line from Liverpool Street, via King's Cross was ostensibly to show LNER connections to East Anglia and the East Coast Main Line respectively, but it also had the effect of underlining the ease with which City workers could reach the stockbroker belt.

typeset. The map suffered as a result, for the typeface chosen by the typesetter was relatively small, and although Gill Sans is remarkably clear, the use of a slightly larger typesize would probably have made the station names a little easier to read from the corner seats.

The Railway Gazette reproduced the map in its issue of 29 August 1932, and this time credited George Dow with its design. The LNER was not so generous, because although it is believed that the company paid him £5 for it, once again it did not let him put his name or initials on the map.

In 1932, therefore, the year before the first Beck Underground map appeared, George Dow had produced four diagrammatic maps[13]. The appearance of the first Beck map may well have been prompted by the forthcoming gathering of all the Underground railways into the London Passenger Transport Board, in July 1933. A common map of all the railways, particularly one in a modern style, was no doubt seen as a most useful unifying tool, both in the mind of the public and of the staff.

Beck had not found it easy to persuade his employer to see the benefit of the diagrammatic principle, even though diagrammatic maps had been used in Underground trains since at least 1920. Apparently the management believed that the public would never accept such a map for the whole system. And yet the evidence was there, not only on the LNER and LMS, but also with the open endorsement of the principal trade railway journal, *The Railway Gazette*. It is tempting to wonder if Beck sought to win approval for his maps by telling his management that LNER passengers had been seeing diagrammatic system maps since 1929, apparently without complaint. Beck had almost certainly seen the LNER maps, for he lived at Highgate and had only to travel once on the LNER line to or from Highgate to see the map in their compartments.

As noted earlier, the Beck Underground map was not constrained by the shape of seat-back picture frames: it appeared first as a pocket folder and then, almost immediately, as a quad royal poster (50″ × 40″), both much deeper formats. In both, the layout of the map could be more generously proportioned on the north–south axis. Not only that, but the need to distinguish between the various lines which made up the Underground required the use of colour printing: this necessity resulted in one of the great visual attractions of the map.

Ken Garland, who has written extensively about the Beck maps has said that although, since he wrote the book, he has been made aware that there were diagrammatic maps in use before the Beck Underground map, he believes that H. C. Beck was the first to use selective scale enlargement (in the area at the east end of the Circle Line, for example) to create space for many lines at the expense of scale on the outer reaches of the system. He referred to it as the convex effect.[14] In fact Beck was not first in this, for many of the route diagrams recorded in this book were laid out with stations at equal distances, and, as an immediate example, the LNER GN

13. The fourth was for the LMS, in 1931, as mentioned in the next chapter.

14. Talk at London's Transport Museum, 6 May 2003.

and GE lines diagrams of 1929 did precisely this. For example at the south end of the GN diagram, each inch of diagram showed 1.67 miles, while at Hitchin (32 miles from London) each inch showed 6.6 miles. Similarly, on the Hertford loop, the stations on the map were a constant 0.75 inches apart even though on the ground they vary from nine-tenths of a mile apart at the south end (Wood Green and Bowes Park) to 3.5 miles apart at the north end (Cuffley and Bayford).

The LNER, no less than London Underground, liked the diagrammatic map and was ready to use it more extensively.

3. Work for the LMS

MANCHESTER, SOUTH JUNCTION & ALTRINCHAM RAILWAY
ROUTE DIAGRAM

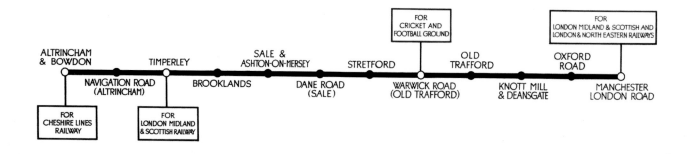

3.1 The MSJ&A route diagram was simple and stylish . . .

The fact that George Dow had produced the first two maps for the LNER in 1929 came to the attention of the London Midland & Scottish Railway. In 1931 he was approached by the LMS to produce a route diagram for the Manchester, South Junction & Altrincham line, which was in the process of being electrified and equipped with new rolling stock. The LNER, part owner of the MSJ&A, gave its consent, and the map [3.1], complete with his initials on it, earned George Dow a commission of £25.

The map was a simple straight-line route diagram, hand-drawn, with twelve stations, of which four were highlighted with rings. Three were interchanges, as a passenger familiar with London maps would have expected, but the fourth was the station for Warwick Road (Old Trafford). This, with a flag, was necessary to draw attention to the need for passengers travelling to Old Trafford for sports fixtures to alight at Warwick Road rather than at the station named Old Trafford itself. This is significant as the first use of a flag to highlight a local attraction on an ordinary general service map. Earlier uses had been restricted to special purpose maps such as the Metropolitan Railway map of 1924 for the British Empire exhibition, and generally on Underground maps to high-light connections. George Dow used them for connections to a greater extent in his 1935 poster map for the LMS, as described below.

To obtain the maximum space for the station names, these were shown alternately above and below the line of route. The lettering was deliberately not the same as that which George Dow had used on the LNER maps. The letters were closely pitched together, though not losing legibility, and some were full of character. The W, for example, which appears seven times on the diagram, comprises two inter-linked Vs. It was a conscious effort to impart a modern feeling to the map.[1]

1. Edward Johnston had used this form of W as an alternative in early versions of his typeface for the Underground, but it was abandoned after a few years.

INTERIOR THIRD-CLASS COMPARTMENT.
[*Courtesy M. S. J. & A. Railway Co.*]

It is not known who on the LMS commissioned the diagram. Very probably the advertising manager Loftus Allen asked the LNER if they could use George Dow's services. A small commemorative leaflet was produced at the time that the electrified services were started, and one of the illustrations therein shows a third class compartment interior complete with its map [3.2]. The LMS, dealing with someone not on its own staff, allowed George Dow to put his initials on the map, and paid him for his effort. More important, perhaps, they printed it from his original, without typesetting.

In 1935 the LMS asked George Dow to produce two further maps. The first was drawn early that year, and its appearance coincided with the rebuilding of Fenchurch Street station[2] and the addition of several new services to the Tilbury and Southend lines operated by the LMS. The map was a carriage panel, and in stylish and distinctive form showed the LMS lines from Fenchurch Street and St Pancras[3] through Southend to Shoeburyness[4] [3.3]. In it George Dow re-introduced the white-line connector, as it has been called, between King's Cross and St Pancras stations, to show their adjacent nature. This form of connector had been used occasionally on London Underground geographical maps, and was eventually introduced to the Underground diagrammatic map eleven years later, in 1946.

The stations are George Dow's customary solid circles, with interchanges (which he called "exchanges" in the Reference panel) as rings. Horizontal lines had, in the main, station names on alternate sides of the line, while lines at common angles were used to very good effect, at 55

3.2 . . . seen here at far right in an MSJ&A third class compartment

2. Owned by the LNER but used extensively by the LMS.

3. Via a change at Kentish Town.

4. The map was published also in *The Railway Gazette* on 8 March 1935. The LMS registered it in their system as ERO 53226.

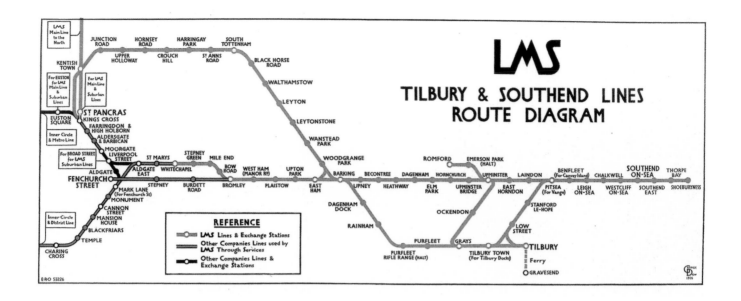

3.3 The LTS route diagram had even more panache.

5. The map was reproduced in *The Railway Gazette* on 27 September 1935. No original poster has yet been traced by the author, and the illustration here is copied from *The Railway Gazette*.

6. On a map of this inclination, at about 63 degrees, the station names could have been at 27 degrees, thus perpendicular to the lines, but this would probably have been regarded as too precious for the supply of basic information to passengers.

degrees either side of the horizontal. They offered more room, and had George Dow's preferred layout of all names on the same side of the line. The ferry service was shown from Tilbury to Gravesend, but the Thames itself, probably regarded as superfluous in the presence of the word *ferry*, was not shown. Dominating the map was a conjoined LMS logo which George Dow designed, in the hope that the LMS would take to it and adopt it for wider use. Alas, they did not, but once again they reproduced the map directly from the original artwork. It was produced on two card sizes, presumably to cater for different sizes of frames in Midland, LT&S, and LMS vehicles.

The second 1935 map was altogether different, for it was for a double royal poster [3.4]. It is not thought that it was prompted by any particular event, but it was unquestionably one of the most stylish George Dow had produced. It showed the London suburban electric lines of the LMS, from Poplar, Broad Street and Euston to Watford Junction, Croxley Green and Rickmansworth. Lines to Kew Bridge, Richmond, Earls Court and Clapham Junction were also shown, and as a through service all the way from Queens Park, to Elephant & Castle, albeit that this was on the Bakerloo tube line. As a result, all three other main line companies are mentioned, as well as five of the Underground lines. Two of the flags mention local attractions. It was a most comprehensive map, aligned up the full space afforded by the double royal layout, at an eye-catching angle of 63 degrees.[5]

It embodies many of the characteristics that George Dow had favoured in earlier maps, not least of which that it was set at an angle, rather than aligned vertically. Station names are in capital letters throughout, although information in flags is in lower case with initial capitals. Station names are all horizontal,[6] and principal stations are in a larger size with

42

correspondingly thicker letter strokes. The copy printed in *The Railway Gazette* is in black and white only, and so it is not known if it embodied any colour. There is a strong chance that it followed the lead of the Tilbury map, with red lines and black lettering.

At six of the stations George Dow again used the white-line connector to join interchange symbols on adjacent lines. Five are pairs and one is a triple. Once again he used the conjoined LMS logo, repeating it six times in the Reference panel and the various flags on the map. In the title of the map, he drew it as outline letters, rather than the solid letters on the Tilbury map. Once again, unfortunately, it did not catch on. But, once again, such was the standard of his drawing, the map was reproduced directly from his original.

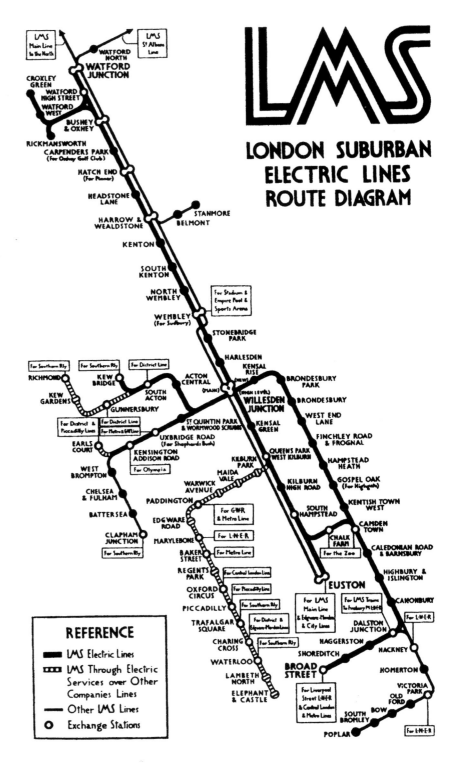

3.4 George Dow produced a superbly elegant map for the LMS in 1935 with his London suburban map.

Reproduced from The Railway Gazette

4. More maps for the LNER

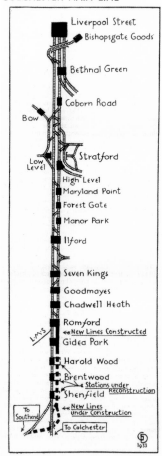

4.1 This map was not intended for public use: it appeared in the LNER Magazine. But it departed from the diagrammatic conventions of style which George Dow was helping to establish in the 1930s.

1. It was the first LNER map upon which he was allowed to place his name, after he had asked Dandridge specifically to allow it. By this time Beck's name was appearing on each new London Underground map. A small point for both men, but not unimportant.

2. The number of diagonal lines was a strong feature of the Beck map from 1933 until 1941, when most of the diagonals were eliminated. They did not return until the Hutchinson-designed map of 1960.

George Dow made progress through a variety of responsibilities on the LNER. In 1931 he had had a brief spell in the Press Section, which only served to whet his appetite for work with the public face of the railway, and from 1932 to 1937 was a District Agent, which title meant that he was a canvasser, selling advertising space on LNER properties, including particularly stations. Also, by this time he was a frequent contributor to the LNER staff magazine.

In early 1933 he drew a route diagram of the lines between Liverpool Street and Shenfield, which were then in the course of widening and station extension [4.1]. The diagram is quite different from all other Dowagrams, and was drawn in a style that recognised that it was destined for publication in the company magazine, rather than as a carriage panel or poster. It appeared in the LNER Magazine in March 1933 and turns geographical mapping more or less on its head, for Liverpool Street is at the top of its vertical line, and Shenfield, actually somewhat north of east, is shown at the bottom. Between them are shown the fast and slow lines, with stations serving the one or the other, or both, and with crossovers, junctions and the new lines all shown. Lines are hatched, stations are solid rectangles. It could hardly be further removed from the style of the GN, GE, and GC Lines maps, and it shows a great ability to devise something new – in today's language, to think outside the box. It can be seen, also, that station names are shown in upper and lower case lettering.

In the same year the LNER introduced diagrammatic posters, as they were called, to show fares from suburban stations on Great Eastern lines. While a common layout was used for all maps on a particular line, at each station different fares information was required to be shown. In an accompanying note in the LNER Magazine for December, mention is that such a map had been introduced "some time ago" on the GN lines. Neither was drawn by George Dow, and they were probably produced locally at the request of the passenger manager.

George Dow was however asked by Cecil Dandridge, the LNER's brilliant advertising manager, to produce a more complex diagrammatic map in 1935 [4.2]. It was, perhaps, inevitable that his three carriage route diagrams should sooner or later have to be drawn together, and the requested map was to show all three LNER lines, GN, GE, and GC, showing them running further from London, for a brochure for selling commercial advertising space.[1] No doubt George Dow's time as a canvasser, in which he may well have visited most if not all of the stations, provided useful knowledge in this task. In this new Dowagram there was no constraint of the seat-back picture frame, and George Dow set all diagonal lines at a constant forty-five degrees.[2] The result was a beautifully

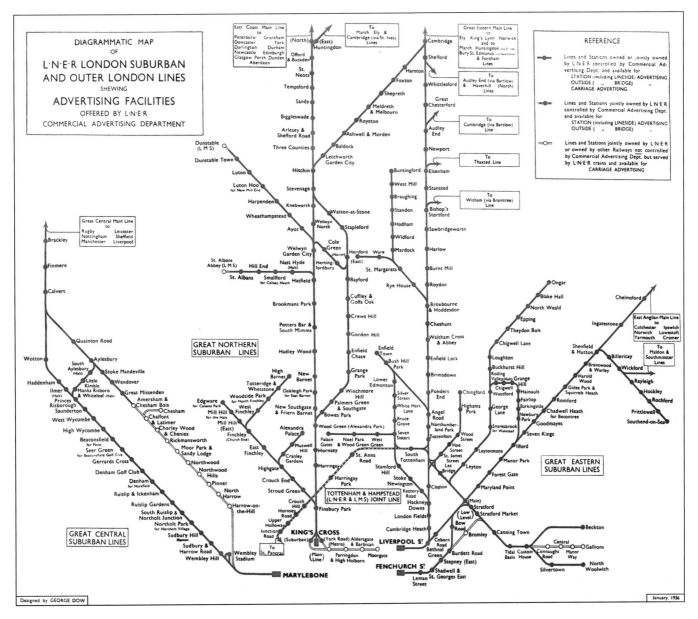

January. 1936

balanced map, almost as symmetrical as one could wish for. However, he did not adopt H. C. Beck's favoured (but not sole) designation for a station, in the form of a short "tick" perpendicular to the line. George Dow remained faithful, then and ever after, to the solid circle.[3] Another innovation, believed to be a first for typeset diagrammatic maps, was the use of lower case letters with initial capitals for station names; in this matter of style it was well ahead of its time. The map was printed with red lines and black station names on a sheet 15″ × 13″, and folded into an orange card cover for presentation to advertisers.

The new map was more extensive than any other he drew for the LNER. It was also more extensive, in incorporating no less than 243

4.2 Cecil Dandridge commissioned this remarkable map from George Dow in 1935 for a brochure aimed at clients of the LNER's commercial advertising department.

3. One of the benefits of the solid or open circle is that all stations are given the same overall shape. LU maps have long used the open circle for interchanges but a tick, on one side of the line, for all others.

stations, than the Beck London Underground map at the time.[4] Its purpose, for the whole of the LNER's London area, and well out into the Home Counties, was to show the commercial advertising facilities available on stations, by the line side, on bridges over roads, and in trains. It was quite an achievement; one measure of its success, in cartographic terms, was that it contains no instances of station names being superimposed on lines.

This all-London LNER map, which appeared in January 1936, was too good and too useful to be used only for selling advertising space to a limited clientele. By 1937 George Dow was working for Dandridge in the LNER's commercial advertising department, devising means of standardising and tidying up many aspects of display, including that of commercial advertising, at stations. He redrew the map to be used in LNER London suburban timetables. This was folded into the back cover, and replaced a geographical map by George Philip & Sons, which map had in turn replaced a map by Bartholomew. He drew in the boundaries of the map, by not including furthermost lines, for these were not covered by what were regarded as suburban services and covered by those timetables [4.3, 4.4]. Against each line was shown the number of the relevant suburban timetable.

He added much information, through simple symbols or pictograms, about parking facilities and attractions local to the stations shown, something which the London Underground map has rarely done. Although he had shown local attractions in square or rectangular flags, attached to the relevant station by a thin line, in the MSJ&A map of 1931 and LMS London electrified lines map of 1935, in this new LNER map he used the device of a small circle containing an illustrative code for each of the various attractions. This avoided the extensive use of text, and allowed strings of three or four circles to be attached to a station where necessary. Indeed, Wembley and Southend each had five circles. This is probably one of the earliest uses of the pictogram in the railway map. He was to revert to the use of the flag on some of the route diagrams developed for the London Midland Region after the war.

This new version of the LNER London suburban map seems to have been prepared in George Dow's own time, even though it was, in effect, official business. The author's mother[5], who at the time worked in the Press Section at King's Cross, once recalled helping to apply the seemingly countless symbols to the design layout for the map in preparation for the typesetter, this task being accomplished on the kitchen table.

In both maps, George Dow nodded to H. C. Beck by using lines set only at the horizontal, vertical, and at 45 degrees. The folded map was at last of a shape which could give room for proper expression of the north-serving LNER lines. The result, in fact, gives the impression of being far more at 45 degrees than the London Underground map ever was. Only

4. H. C. Beck showed nearly this number on his map of 1937, albeit that several were on lines under construction. But Beck had taken a while to avoid superimposing station names on lines, and he always had difficulty in showing the east end of the District Line, showing several stations in a flag. He did not overcome this problem, and manage to show the full system, until 1954, twenty-one years after his first map appeared.

5. Doris Soundy, who had joined the LNER in April 1926, and who married George Dow in March 1940.

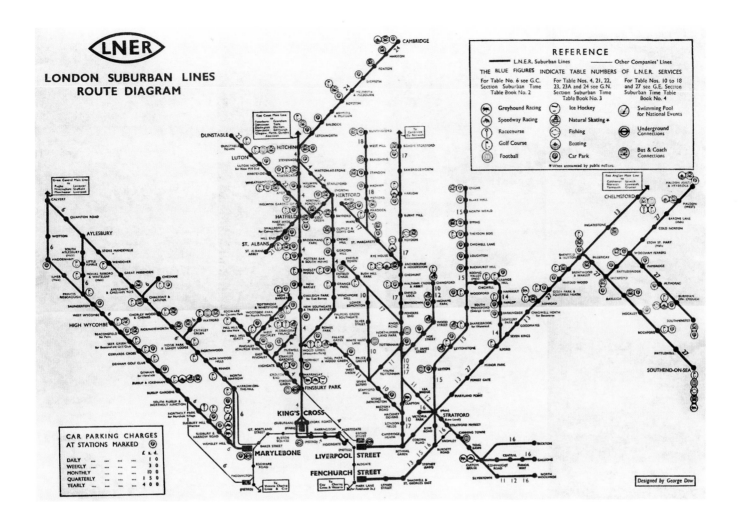

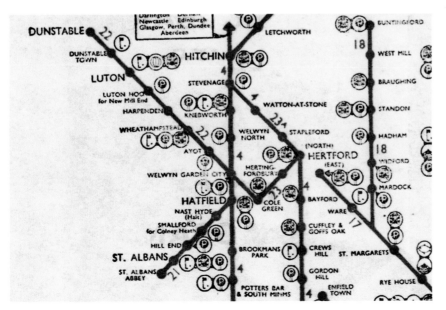

4.3 Here George Dow used the basic format of the 1935 advertising map, in a revised version for the LNER London suburban timetables; in doing so he outdid Beck in the use of 45 degree diagonals.

4.4 Detail of the London suburban map to show the use of pictograms at stations and timetable numbers beside the lines. This is shown approximately full size. The poor printing quality is on the original.

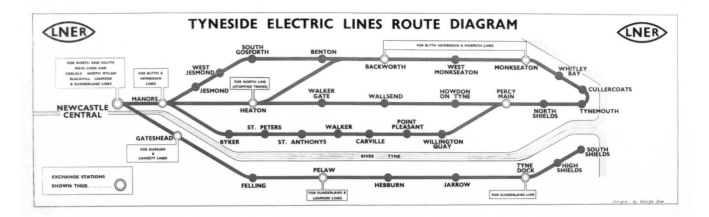

TYNESIDE ELECTRIC LINES ROUTE DIAGRAM

4.5 The LNER introduced new stock on the Tyneside lines, and equipped them with two versions of this map, shown here with the line to South Shields shown . . .

4.6 . . . in one of the trains, from an advertising brochure.

6. Although, after the war, the LNER continued to use this map in a simplified form, in Chapter 7 will be found mention of a redesign used by the Eastern Region of British Railways designed by, of all people, H. C. Beck. For some reason he destroyed its symmetry.

four principal lines are vertical, while twenty four lines, long or short, are at a common angle. Virtually nothing is horizontal, and in this writer's opinion, this second version, used in suburban timetables, was every bit as elegant as the early Beck Underground maps.[6] It is a matter of opinion whether it needed different colours on the routes to make it truly pretty, or whether its use of a shade very close to the Garter Blue used on the LNER's incomparable streamline locomotives was elegance enough. Station names were rendered in capital letters throughout, and it was printed on a sheet 14½″ × 10½″ with black lettering and blue lines on a white ground.

The following year, 1938, saw a further essay in diagrammatic maps for rolling stock. The North Tyneside lines, some of which had been long since electrified, were added to by the electrification of the line from

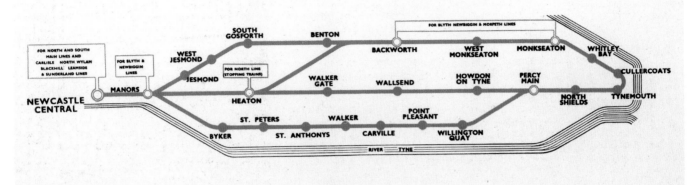

TYNESIDE L·N·E·R ELECTRIC LINES ROUTE DIAGRAM

Newcastle to South Shields. New stock was built for both north and south of the Tyne, and all were fitted with a diagrammatic carriage panel map designed by George Dow in two forms [4.5]. One showed the lines both north and south of the river; the other showed only those to the north [4.7]. They were typeset in Gill Sans, and showed the river, the LNER "Gill"[7] logo, and bore George Dow's customary solid circles and concentric rings for ordinary and interchange stations respectively. They were displayed above eye level on bulkheads between seating areas, across the open cars, and were thus highly visible [4.6].

Seen in the context of later maps drawn of the Tyneside services, George Dow's 1938 map is beautifully symmetrical, with or without the line to South Shields. It is simple and elegant, and certainly suggests that the current Newcastle Metro maps might benefit from a review of their layout on 1938 principles.

The two last LNER diagrams which are known to bear George Dow's name were produced for publicity brochures for Grimsby & Immingham (1938) [4.9] and Hull (1939) [4.8]. They are shown over the centre-page spread in each brochure, and show the railway routes of most of the LNER system converging on the ports, on the left, and the sea routes from them to northern continental Europe on the right. The Hull map is a little more refined, with more parallel arrangement of lines, but both show straight lines imposed upon a geographical coastline. The entire main line from London to Berwick is shown in a straight line.

Similar brochures for other LNER ports, of which there were many, are not thought to have been produced. It is possible that they were planned but abandoned upon the outbreak of war.

4.7 The version without the South Shields line.

7. Not strictly the logo designed by Eric Gill for the LNER; his original had conjoined letters, and this version was given only limited exposure by the LNER before it was redesigned with the four initials rendered separately.

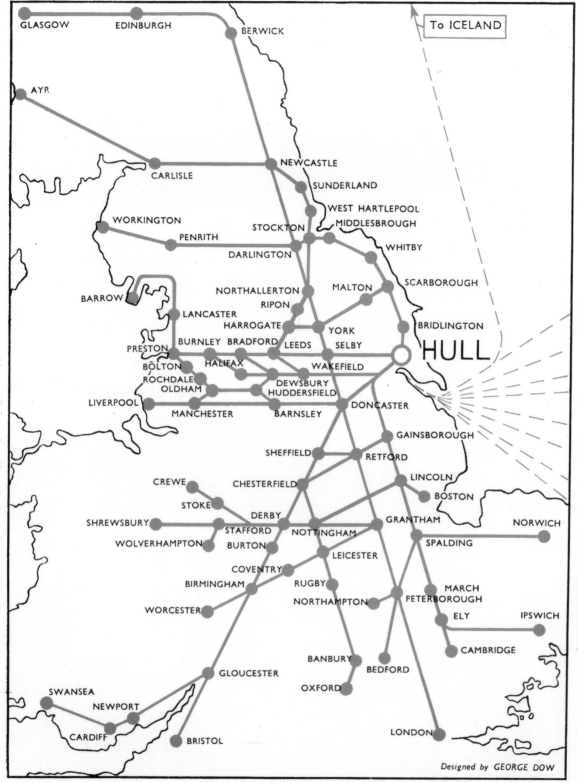

To ICELAND

GLASGOW EDINBURGH BERWICK

AYR

CARLISLE NEWCASTLE
SUNDERLAND
WEST HARTLEPOOL
WORKINGTON STOCKTON MIDDLESBROUGH
PENRITH
DARLINGTON WHITBY
SCARBOROUGH
NORTHALLERTON MALTON
BARROW RIPON
LANCASTER BRIDLINGTON
HARROGATE YORK
PRESTON BURNLEY BRADFORD LEEDS SELBY
HALIFAX WAKEFIELD HULL
BOLTON
ROCHDALE DEWSBURY
OLDHAM HUDDERSFIELD
LIVERPOOL DONCASTER
MANCHESTER BARNSLEY
GAINSBOROUGH
SHEFFIELD RETFORD
LINCOLN
CHESTERFIELD BOSTON
CREWE
STOKE NORWICH
SHREWSBURY DERBY GRANTHAM
STAFFORD NOTTINGHAM SPALDING
WOLVERHAMPTON BURTON
LEICESTER MARCH
COVENTRY PETERBOROUGH
BIRMINGHAM RUGBY ELY IPSWICH
NORTHAMPTON
WORCESTER CAMBRIDGE
BANBURY BEDFORD
SWANSEA GLOUCESTER
OXFORD
NEWPORT
CARDIFF LONDON
BRISTOL

Designed by GEORGE DOW

4.8 Three of
the LNER's
many east coast
ports were
advertised by
means of
brochures,
each of which
contained a
diagrammatic
map of railway
and steamship
services to
Scandinavia,
Baltic ports
and northern
Europe, shown
in much the
same style as
on the
Immingham/
Grimsby map,
opposite. This
one featured
Hull. 1939.

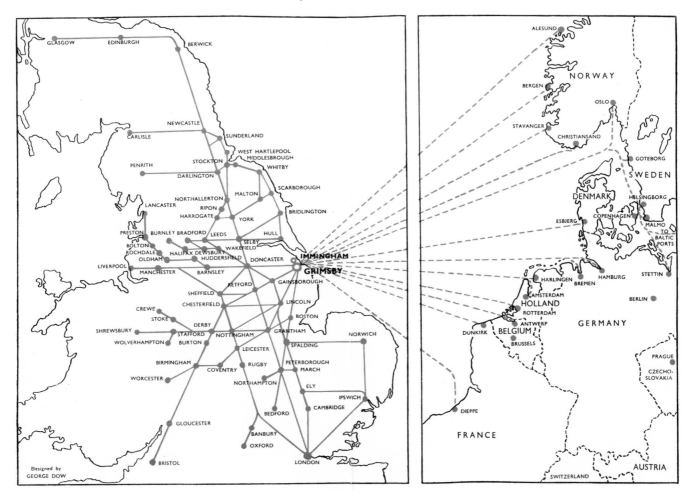

It was then that the route diagram inside carriages became so important: station name signs were removed during the invasion threat, and passengers had ever more need to have a developed sense of where they were at any time. The LNER suburban passenger in London and on Tyneside was better off than most.

4.9 Grimsby and Immingham shared a 1938 brochure, which contained this map.

5. A brief diversion

In 1941 George Dow came close to trespassing upon H.C. Beck's territory, in a sense. On 14 June 1941 the London evening newspaper *The Star* published an article by him. This was to advocate a forward look to peace, when he expected there to be the opportunity to reduce the number of mainline stations in London while providing better services for passengers. He was very much aware that London had no Union Station, in the American style. His proposals contemplated the construction of tunnels to allow railway connections to be made east–west (Paddington to Liverpool Street) and north–south (in the area of Euston/King's Cross to Charing Cross) with the lines crossing at a new station north of Tottenham Court Road. He was also proposed a line from Marylebone/Paddington to Victoria.

Much of the thrust of these proposals was to call for faster cross-capital transit, through fewer changes, than was available on ever-longer tube lines. All of this was accompanied by a characteristically elegant diagrammatic map bearing the initials GD.

The article ran thus:

In the London of the future railway and tube facilities must be drastically re-planned.

This was clearly shown in "The Star" when an American Architect, Mr. C Howard Crane, suggested that the capital might well be served by two or three main railway stations, instead of the present dozen or so terminals.

Presupposing the electrification of all lines, he advocated as examples, the combination of King's Cross, St Pancras and Euston on the one hand, and Victoria, Waterloo, Charing Cross and Cannon Street on the other.

An admirable suggestion. By all means have the terminals of the main line railways reduced by combination to three, four or five, to deal with the provincial and long distance trains, but let us avoid the error of perpetuating any of them for suburban working.

I am convinced that the London suburban lines cannot play their full part in meeting, together with London Transport, the travelling demands of the capital until they have been interconnected across the central area and electrified. The present situation is the same as if the Piccadilly Tube only operated northwards from a terminal at King's Cross and southwards from Green Park or, if you like, the Edgware-Morden ran northwards from a Warren-street terminal and southwards from the Strand.

In short, our suburban railway terminals should be in the outer zone of Greater London, as is the case with practically all of the Underground lines, and not in the fringes of the central area.

It is not overlooked that, but for the war, some immense schemes of electrification and tube projection would have been almost completed by now. These include the electrification of the L.N.E.R. from Liverpool-street and Fenchurch-street to Shenfield, and the projection of the Central tube eastwards over the

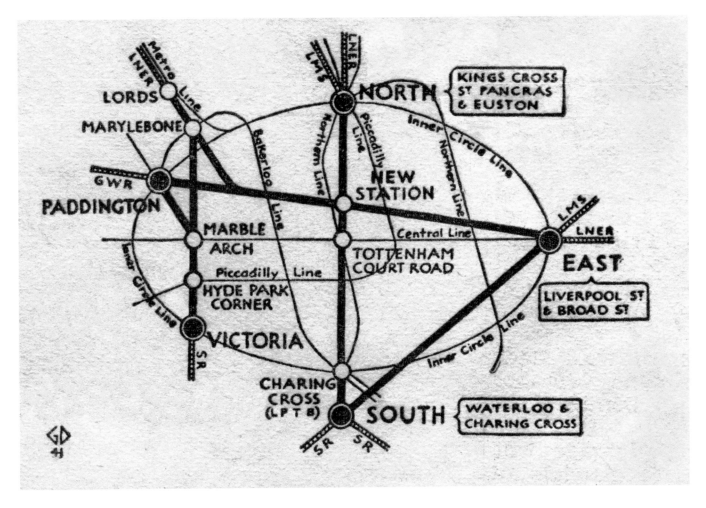

L.N.E.R. to Ongar and Newbury Park, and westwards alongside the Great Western and L.N.E.R. from North Acton to Ruislip.

The last-named scheme will give a record through Tube service of 39 miles from Ruislip to Ongar, the longest at present being from High Barnet to Morden, a distance of 21 miles, with 30 intermediate stations.

Now such a tube service is admirable for the comparatively short journey from Archway to Angel, or Balham to Bank, but would you not prefer a speedier alternative for a journey from Northolt to North Weald?

In any further schemes for the projection of the Tubes over the suburban railways, let it therefore first be considered whether better alternative services can be given by a replanning of the suburban railways themselves.

Let us have existing transport facilities improved (to include the re-siting of certain suburban stations) and the bad districts of the central and outer central areas redesigned and rebuilt before London is encouraged or allowed to sprawl farther afield.

Let us see that done before we create new dormitory areas, to the detriment of the Green Belt, by the extension of new tubes.

Let us therefore have the admirable Southern electric system radiating from Waterloo linked with the L.M.S. electric lines at Broad Street and the presently

5.1 George Dow's wartime suggestions for new peacetime stations and cross-London services were illustrated by this distinctive diagrammatic map, enlarged from its original appearance in print.

From The London Evening Star

53

electrified lines of the L.N.E.R. out of Liverpool Street by means of an extended and enlarged Waterloo and City Tube. This would give the traveller from Staines to Broxbourne or from Shenfield to Guildford a fast journey with not more than one simple change.

Let us have tunnels driven between Lords station and Victoria, with a spur to Paddington and intermediate Tube exchange stations at Marylebone, Marble Arch and Hyde Park Corner. Here the Southern would be linked with the Great Western, L.N.E.R., and the Metropolitan line, and rapid journeys between Watford and Dorking, or Gerrards Cross and Croydon, could be made with one change at most.

Other, equally useful links spring to mind. A new North Station, created from King's Cross, St Pancras and Euston could be joined to Charing Cross, with a Tube exchange station on the way at Tottenham Court-road. An invaluable East-West connection would be provided by a tunnel linking Liverpool-street and Broad-street with Paddington and Marylebone, possessing an interchange station with the proposed North-South line at the point of intersection.

Such suburban line connections are not impracticable suggestions. They would relieve the tube lines of an enormous amount of interchange traffic. They would considerably reduce travelling time across the capital, as intermediate stops would be few. They would form short, invaluable links between the main line railways, for they could also be used for urgent freight traffic, hauled of course, by electric locomotives.

Perhaps it was extraordinary that space should be given to such a proposal at the darkest days of the War, but it was probably the newspaper's way of indicating that the nation had to assume that it would win, and would wish to bring improvements to the capital after victory[1].

The context, at the time that the article was written, was that the nation, and in particular London, had just sustained the most extensive and prolonged attack by aerial bombardment the world had ever known. In it many stations, including King's Cross, where George Dow had his office in pre-war days, was among those badly damaged, and it was not then known whether more was to come.[2] It was therefore not then known how much reconstruction would have to be undertaken.

The proposals were illustrated by the simple diagrammatic map shown. It has been copied from George Dow's press cuttings book, on yellowing wartime newsprint, and given some cleaning, electronically, before reproduction here. It is typical of George Dow's draughtsmanship: hand drawn, bold lines, a mix of lettering sizes to suit various needs, and all close to the Gill Sans typeface that he so admired. It will be seen that he quite ignored the diagrammatic conventions so recently established by his work for the LNER, and by Beck's work for LPTB. He used lines of two thicknesses, shied away from the geometrically regular, and did not hesitate to use an oval amidst a number of straight lines. The thick lines were those he suggested be built; the thin lines were those in existence but which emphasised the need for the proposed lines. In a map of this kind, geometric regularity was not as important as giving an instant picture of

1. The article subsequently received favourable editorial comment in both *Modern Transport* (21 June 1941) and the *Railway Gazette* (4 July 1941).

2. It did, in the V1 and V2 attacks in 1944.

relative position. And the function of the oval, to represent the far-from-circular Circle Line, served to hold all of the other lines together.[3]

It is the earliest known map on which he applied his initials GD in a diamond-shaped monogram, and which he used ever thereafter.

In hindsight, it is interesting to see that while the connection between Euston and Charing Cross was first mooted in the 1860s, to secure access to the Channel ports for the LNWR via the South Eastern Railway, the east–west proposal appears to have been new. Certainly the proposal for both simultaneously, with new termini, appears to have been wholly new. Both north–south and east–west proposals were echoed in the late 1980s when the Crossrail project was conceived. The north–south element found limited expression, without the new termini or the interchange station, in Thameslink services, and the east–west Paddington–Liverpool Street element remains as a good intention and rather a political football today, more than sixty years after George Dow's proposal in a wartime London evening newspaper.

3. Whether or not this feature was consciously taken from the Metropolitan map of 1921 is not known.

6. London Midland Region maps, 1949–1955

6.1 Harlequin produced this view of George Dow, the artist, when he was Public Relations & Publicity Officer of the London Midland Region, 1952.

1. In 1944; both titles were a little inadequate; the job involved responsibility for all aspects of public relations for the LNER.

2. The all-London suburban map remained in LNER London suburban timetables for the remainder of the company's existence. Some changes were made after the war to reflect the availability of services, and in the last (6 October 1947 ufn), the attractions symbols were removed, some extremities of the lines lopped off, and the reference to George Dow's having designed it removed.

3. The LMS in England and Wales had not been cut into two regions as the LNER had. The LM was thus the largest BR Region.

4. The first of these showed steam, electric and diesel trains at Bushey; the second showed passenger and mineral trains on the Woodhead line, recently electrified.

George Dow's promotion to Information Agent on the LNER in June 1939 (re-titled Press Relations Officer later[1]), and then the outbreak of war, put a stop to any further hours at the drawing board. Changes to his designs by other hands were inevitable, but there was no time to be concerned about that.[2] For a little more than a year after the creation of British Railways in 1948 he was Public Relations & Publicity Officer of the Eastern & North Eastern Regions of British Railways, during which period he wrote a small book about the electrification of the line from Liverpool Street to Shenfield. Within is a diagrammatic map almost identical with the eastern part of that shown on page 79. Its appearance in the booklet in late 1949 suggests that the timetable map shown at **7.2** was originally drawn earlier that year.

In April 1949, in the second year of the new British Railways, George Dow moved to Euston as Public Relations & Publicity Officer of the London Midland Region.[3] He took much experience from the LNER with him, and in his six years in charge of London Midland public relations he brought about the extensive use of the diagrammatic map in trains and on posters. Indeed, the London Midland probably made more extensive use of diagrammatic maps on stations and in trains than any other part of British Railways.

In this work he used the services of a projectionist on his staff at Euston House. When interviewed by his new chief, Vic Welch had declared an interest in drawing and illustration, and was put to work by George Dow, producing a dozen or more diagrammatic maps and their variations, for use in the rolling stock of the region's electric services, and then more complex designs in the form of double royal posters for display at stations in nine or ten areas of the Region. He was then set to producing pictorial posters, of which the best known were *Trains of Our Times* and *Britain's First All-Electric Railway*.[4] He must have enjoyed this more than being a projectionist with occasional spells at the drawing board, for not long afterwards he left British Railways to become a highly successful freelance railway artist.

When he went to Euston, George Dow found that the former LMS had been a little slow in keeping many aspects of information design up to date. The regional public relations and publicity officers on British Railways were given more extensive powers than their predecessors on the four main line companies had held. As well as the core tasks of keeping the press (regarded separately as National, Provincial, and Technical) well informed of all railway matters, they included not only advertising but more particularly station displays, and information for passengers throughout their journeys. There were also responsibilities for displays in

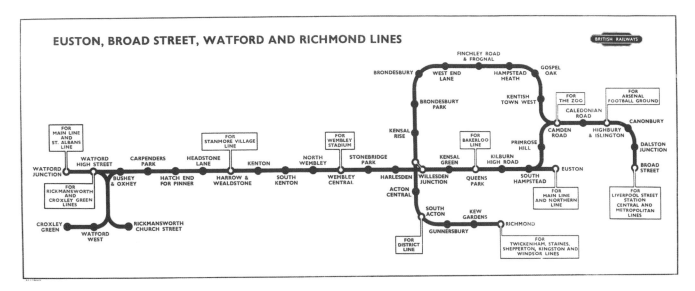

EUSTON, BROAD STREET, WATFORD AND RICHMOND LINES

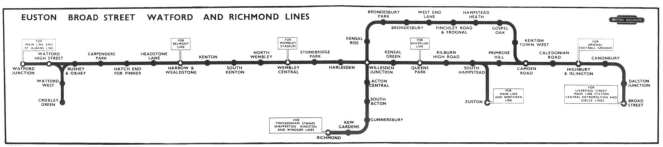

EUSTON   BROAD STREET   WATFORD   AND RICHMOND LINES

carriages, particularly the pictorial items above seatbacks in compartments, and route diagrams. George Dow's substantial budget allowed him to tackle the errors of omission of the LMS, many of which had been made worse by the removal of most station name signs during the war.

He launched an extensive programme of work, across a wide range of London Midland stations, designed to provide improved signage. This included not only the familiar name signs within the British Railways totem, but many other items specific to the stations as well as generic items such as hanging signs, doorplates and posterboard headings. Directional signs, within and without stations, were an important part of the whole task.

Within his responsibility for displays in passenger rolling stock, George Dow commissioned three series of pictorial carriage panels, including one on railway architecture and the well-known historical views by Hamilton Ellis. On seven electrified lines he charged Vic Welch with producing diagrammatic route maps for display in the dedicated rolling stock with which they were equipped. Most of them, as can be seen, were fairly simple, and none of them sought to break new ground in their design: they had to be in what was by now a familiar language.[5] Broadly, they were of two different types. Two were printed on card, and were of modest

6.2 The London Midland Region series of route diagrams, designed by Vic Welch to the requirements of George Dow, started with a new look at the Euston, Broad Street, Watford and Richmond lines George Dow had put into his 1935 poster for the LMS. On card, ERO 53226/6

6.3 This paper version of the Euston, Broad Street, Watford and Richmond lines does not include Rickmansworth and shows Euston as a branch. BR 35019/18

5. The design and general layout was much the same as that of the simple route diagram used in the Eastern Region's Liverpool Street-Shenfield electric trains, for which George Dow was almost certainly responsible in late 1948 or early 1949, before he went to Euston in April of that year.

This is the handed pair of Manchester and Bury line diagrams. Both are on paper and have the same ERO number, 53577/10.

6.4 Manchester Victoria at right;
6.5 Manchester Victoria at left

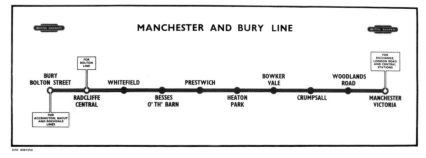

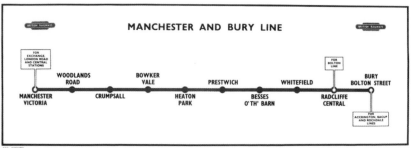

size. The use of card is good evidence (but not proof) that they were used to replace other maps, in frames, within compartment stock. All of the others were printed on paper, and were somewhat larger. This combination is even stronger proof that they were for use in carriages that did not have frames used for earlier maps, and that they were to be pasted to the lower ceiling of open saloon cars. All of the maps were to a common house style in symbology and overall design. The London maps and the MSJ&A map, as described below, incorporated flags to show local attractions, but this device was not used extensively across the region.

The Euston and Broad Street lines commanded a lot of attention. In the office file of reference copies are four versions of the Euston lines map. The sequence in which they were prepared is not known. Two were on light card, for insertion in frames in compartment stock.[6] The larger of the two bears a black border and the reference number ERO53226/6[7] [6.2], while the smaller has no border and no reference number. It may have been a draft. Both are extensively flagged for connecting services, and ERO53226/6 includes the line from Watford and Bushey to Rickmansworth. There are also a few flags for attractions. The white-line connector is used at Willesden Junction, and also within the "poles" for flags, to draw the eye to the information therein. Gill Sans, standard for British Railways, is used throughout. Other than minor differences in layout, principally to allow the map to cover a larger area of the card on ERO53226/6, the two maps are essentially the same.

Altogether larger were two paper maps, pasted on the lower ceilings of saloon cars. Both were given the reference BR No 35019/18, [6.3], and the only difference between them is that details of connecting services, within flags, are shown in Gill Sans Light and Gill Sans Medium. This change

6. There is a photograph, reproduced in O S Nock's *Britain's Railways at War*, 1971, which shows a wartime LMS suburban compartment under subdued lighting for air-raid conditions. It is thought to have been steam-hauled stock. Dimly seen, pasted to the roof of the compartment, is a diagrammatic map of the electrified lines from Broad Street and Euston. Most of the detail is indiscernible, but the two termini are at the left (presumably on the basis that it would be read from left to right), and consequently with the lines south of Willesden at the top. Its date can only be guessed at, but is probably late 1930s. All stations are shown as rings, and the layout of the routes is not very elegant.

7. Date stamped 19 July 1950 on the rear.

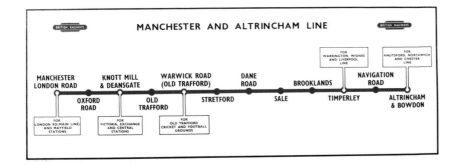

6.6 Manchester and Altrincham line on card. ERO 53226-4

was probably to enhance legibility, and it is reasonable to assume that the Medium version was the later of the two. However it is the former of these varieties of which four examples survive in the preserved LNWR Oerlikon vehicle in the National Railway Museum.

The Manchester–Bury line had four maps also, and all were on paper. ERO 53577/10 was produced in handed pairs [6.4 and 6.5], thus allowing the map to be displayed appropriately with Bury towards the north end of the car, and Manchester Victoria at the south, on both sides of the cars. This allowed the stations to be shown in the same order as they were called on.[8] BR 35019/14 had Bury at the right end, and moved the Bolton connection from Bury to Radcliffe Central. ERO 53226-1 ran on beyond Bury to Holcombe Brook. This presumably was used in other rolling stock, and shows the inherent flexibility of the diagrammatic map, in ease of adjustment to add or remove lines. All four of the Manchester–Bury maps are simple straight-line route diagrams.

Manchester was, of course, the terminal of the old MSJ&A line, subject of George Dow's first commission for the LMS, in 1931. For this line Vic Welch (who almost certainly referred to his chief's copy of the 1931 diagram) reversed the layout, with Manchester London Road at the left end [6.6]. He added a flag for connections at Knott Mill and Deansgate, but otherwise the map is essentially the same as the 1931 map, including the flag for Old Trafford sports ground at Warwick Road. It was produced on card, and presumably fitted in the original frames from 1931.[9]

Another simple straight-line route diagram served the electrified services on the line from Manchester London Road to Hadfield and Glossop. This had been planned for electrification in LNER days, and very probably George Dow would have been called upon to produce a route diagram for it had this happened. It is a simple map, with no reference number, and ending beyond Hadfield with an arrow to other destinations *en route* to Sheffield Victoria.

The other centre of electrified services on the London Midland was Merseyside. The lines from Liverpool Exchange to Southport and Ormskirk, first electrified by the Lancashire & Yorkshire Railway early in the twentieth century, were treated to ERO 53226/5 [6.7], which was produced early enough to include a connection (at Seaforth & Litherland) to

8. It is not known whose idea this was, nor where it was first used. It can only be done where there is no risk of the cars being turned, but it undoubtedly is of assistance to the traveller. On the London Underground the device was used in the streamlined tube cars of 1936 on the Piccadilly line. Today, the route diagrams on the Bakerloo, Jubilee and Victoria lines are all handed, but the Piccadilly can no longer use them because of the loop at Heathrow, which causes trains to be turned.

9. But it should be noted that specimen held by the author is 25″ long, while the 1931 MSJ&A map by George Dow was printed on card only 24″ long. The height of both was 10″.

6.7 Full circle. The Liverpool Southport and Ormskirk lines, subject of the 1904 L&Y semi–diagrammatic route map, on paper.

ERO 53226/5

6.8 Mersey and Wirral lines on paper. ERO 53226-2

6.9 The unusual Lancaster Morecambe and Heysham Electric lines diagram, showing reversals at each intermediate station, on paper. BR 35019/19

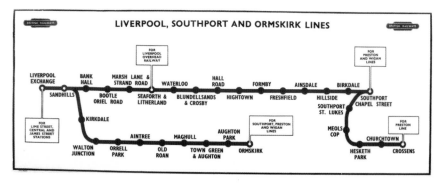

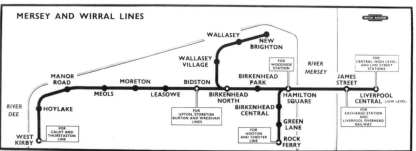

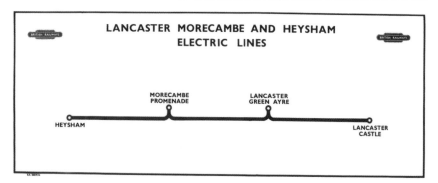

the Liverpool Overhead Railway before it closed.[10] Comparison with the original L&Y map shows a few new stations, and the odd change of name, but the requirement for a simple map, quickly and easily read, had not changed in fifty years. A second version of this map, under the same ERO number, was produced to delete the connection between Marsh Lane and Aintree, through Linacre Road and Ford.[11]

The Mersey and Wirral lines had three maps. ERO 53226-2 was a small version [6.8]. The first version of ERO 53226-3 was vast, at a full five feet long, and like ERO 53226-2 included a reference to Storeton in the flag of connections available at Bidston. It was essentially the same but with a few minor rearrangements of the lines. Storeton was closed in December 1951, and a second version of the large map deleted the reference.

The last of the London Midland route diagrams to be mentioned was the smallest, showing only four stations. The Lancaster Heysham and Morecambe lines, shown in BR 35019/16 [6.9], required trains to reverse at both intermediate stations, and had this feature shown on the map.

10. The LoR had used this to provide direct services to Aintree racecourse for many years.

11. Linacre Road was closed in April 1951, but the line itself allowed the LoR to serve Aintree.

Presumably this was to assure passengers that all was well, even though the train may not have seemed to know which way it was going. It was an interesting piece of information passed on simply and diagrammatically, and certainly smacked of George Dow's eye for detail.

The other major work undertaken by Vic Welch was the design of diagrammatic area maps for display on double royal posters at stations. For these there was no need to restrict the maps to electrified services only. Virtually the whole of the London Midland Region was represented, in an unusual effort to show very extensive main line railways in diagrammatic form. As far as is known ten posters were produced. There is circumstantial evidence that there was an eleventh, but a copy of it has not been found.[12] It is not thought that any were re-issued to reflect changes in the railway, or station closures, and as a result the maps were never developed in the remarkable way that has happened with others, such as the London Underground map.

The London suburban lines were shown with the Euston and St Pancras lines combined in a single map, vertical in alignment, and going as far north as Bletchley and Bedford [6.10]. The inherent flexibility of the diagrammatic form can be seen in the complete lack of similarity between the Euston lines on this map and those on the route diagram illustrated earlier. And yet they both gave the same information, and were equally easy to read.

Bedford and Bletchley also appeared at the south of the map covering the south Midlands, entitled *Bedford Rugby Coventry and Northampton District Lines* [6.11]. Vertical, horizontal and forty-five degree lines predominate but the map loses its shape a little in the area of Coventry.

The East Midlands were covered by a map entitled *Derby Leicester and Nottingham Lines* [6.12]. The Midland main line ran vertically up through the map, with intertwinings of other Midland lines and the old Great Central on the right and other Midland lines, including that from the South West at bottom right and to Buxton, at top left. The map was busy and with hindsight one can see places where it might have been simplified. For example in two or three places lines cross and re-cross each other, but it was not necessary to show this on the map: comprehension would not have been lost without it.[13]

The industrial heart of the Midlands was shown on two maps, *South Staffordshire and Birmingham Lines* [6.13], and *North Staffordshire and South Cheshire Lines* [6.14]. Both were fairly simple, with the former dominated by diagonal lines, and the latter by vertical lines. Certainly George Dow and Vic Welch were open-minded about design and did not feel obliged to follow a single style slavishly. Influences from George Dow in these and the other LM poster maps can be seen in the preference for station names on one side of the line only, but only on the London maps are interchange stations designated by means of a ring. One might have

12. I am indebted to Stan Friedman for help in identifying these maps. George Dow's account of the work undertaken during his time as PR & PO at Euston refers to the production of these maps as part of the great effort to ensure that LM passengers were kept well informed. Stan Friedman has identified nine posters in the series ERO 35018/1 to /10, but has not found /9 of that series. All the others are reproduced here from the copies held by Stan Friedman, as well as one other un-numbered map. As this map duplicated much information on ERO 35018/10, it is not thought to be the missing /9.

13. Indeed, these features could possibly have told the passenger things of which he was not previously aware.

6.10 One of two maps for the
London area: London Midland
London Suburban Lines. BR
35018/10

Stan Friedman collection

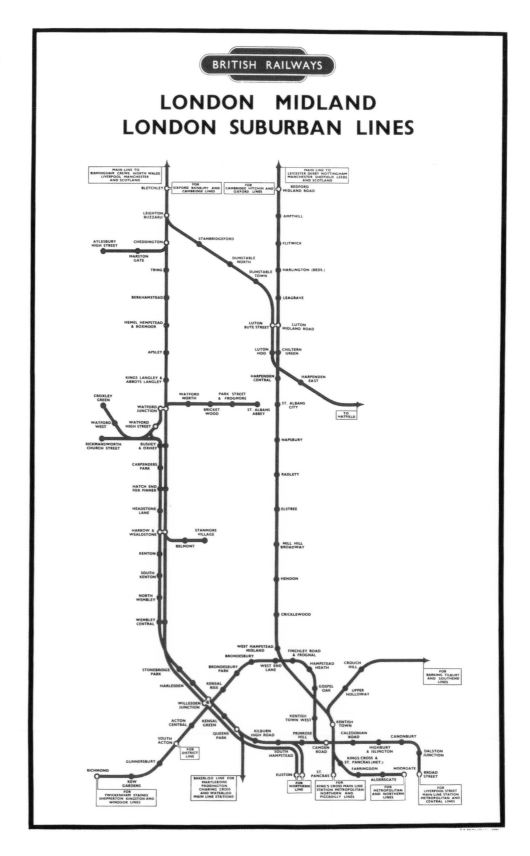

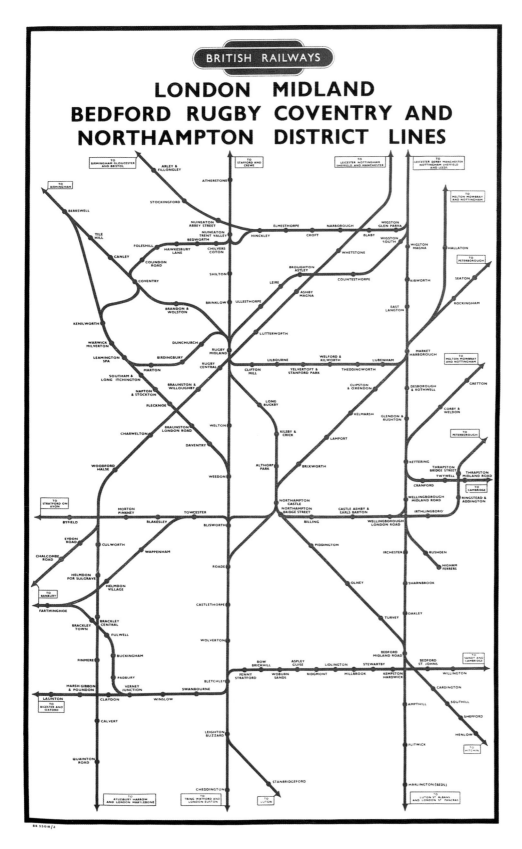

6.11 Bedford Rugby Coventry and Northampton District Lines included the former Great Central route from London. BR 35018/2

Stan Friedman collection

6.12 A touch of spaghetti in the east: Derby Leicester and Nottingham Lines. BR 35018/6

Stan Friedman collection

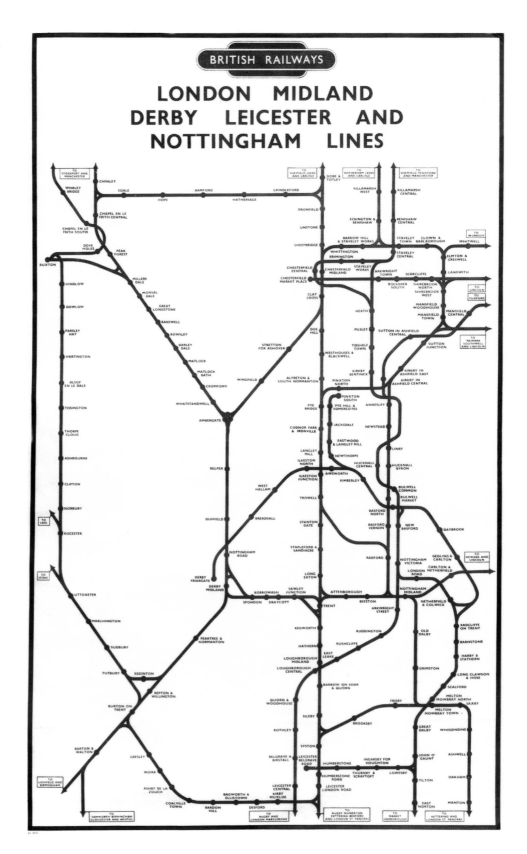

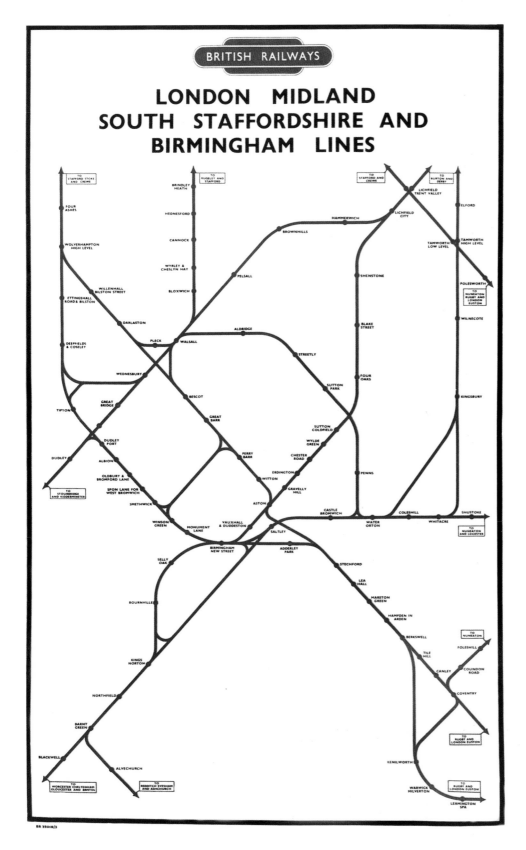

6.13 Strong diagonals marked the South Staffordshire and Birmingham Lines diagram. BR 35018/3

Stan Friedman collection

6.14 North Staffordshire and South Cheshire Lines. BR 35018/4

Stan Friedman collection

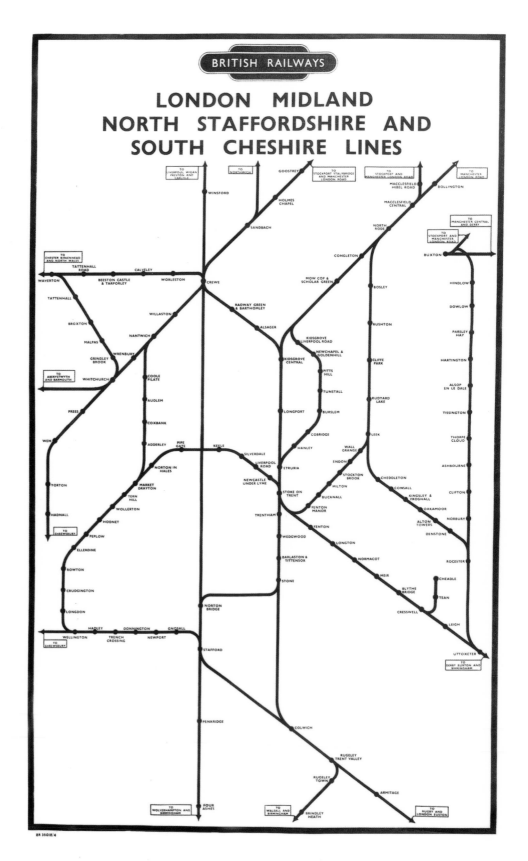

expected junction stations elsewhere to be shown as interchanges, but to have done so would have implied a quick connection, and the timetable did not necessarily offer this.

At the same time we can see Vic Welch's inclinations as an artist. His paintings, familiar to railway enthusiasts, were known for great fidelity and almost clinical precision. This trait can be seen on the *North Staffordshire and South Cheshire Lines* map on the line through the stations at New-chapel & Goldenhill, and at Kidsgrove Liverpool Road. A dedicated diagrammicist would have drawn the line straight north, to meet the Macclesfield line much closer to Mow Cop & Scholar Green. This would have avoided the reverse curve north of Pitts Hill and would have resulted in a simpler map.

The *North Wales Lines* map was a predominantly vertical and horizontal map, and truly diagrammatic in the sense that it completely ignored geography and showed the east–west line along the North Wales coast vertically [6.15]. The coastline itself was also shown, but only to give a point of reference, and certainly not with any geographical fidelity.

Lancashire was covered by three maps, of which two were very busy and not wholly satisfactory. *South West Lancashire and West Cheshire Lines* is the more elegant [6.16], with the West Coast main line straight as a ramrod on the right (a case of diagrammatic presentation giving a sense of directness, if ever there was one), and many of the lines sloping left and right in sympathy with the coastline on the left. *South East Lancashire and Manchester Lines* is less elegant, and faintly resembling a "bowl of wet spaghetti", as an American railroad map was once described[14] [6.17]. The problem was that there seemed to be no unifying feature on which all else could hang, as in the case of the West Coast Main Line or the coast in the South West Lancashire map.

The coast also played a part in giving shape to the *Cumberland Westmorland and North Lancashire Lines* map [6.18]. This has a pleasant open feeling to it, with lines clinging to the coast and the West Coast Main Line again almost entirely straight.

The map that is thought to be missing from this series is ERO 35018/9, but it is not known what it showed. It is possible that the number was reserved in case any regional boundary changes made it necessary. A candidate was the suburban lines from Marylebone. The *Bedford Rugby &c* map, [6.11] illustrated on page 63, showed the ex-Great Central main line in the Midlands, and a route diagram dated 1953 shows the southern end of this line. It refers to "Eastern Region services" but the map is drawn in London Midland maroon, not dark blue, as used on other Eastern Region maps. The significance of these points is not known, but it is noted that the transfer of the Great Central line from the Eastern to the London Midland was discussed for some time before it was finally put into effect in 1959.

14. The Chicago & North Western Railroad, by an anonymous official, quoted by H Roger Grant in *North Western, 1996.*

6.15 The BR 35018 series of double royal maps for display at stations started with North Wales Lines, with the maximum diagrammatic licence of the east-west coast shown vertically. BR 35018/1

Stan Friedman collection

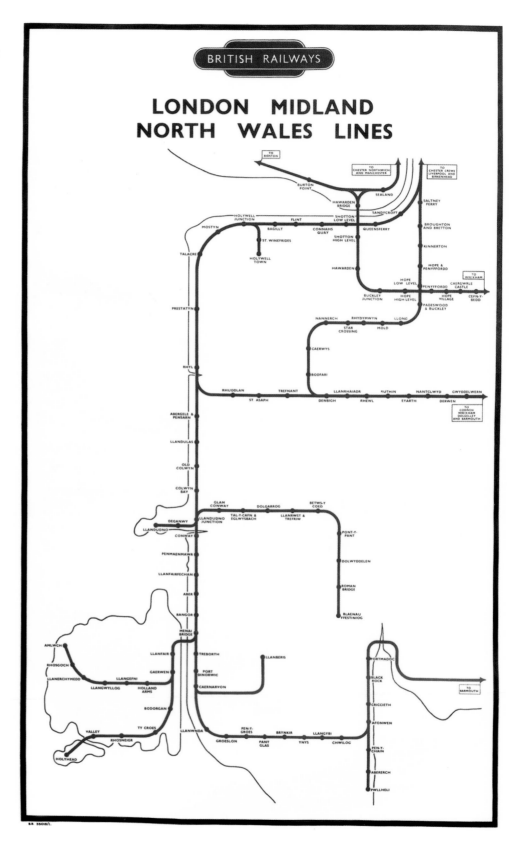

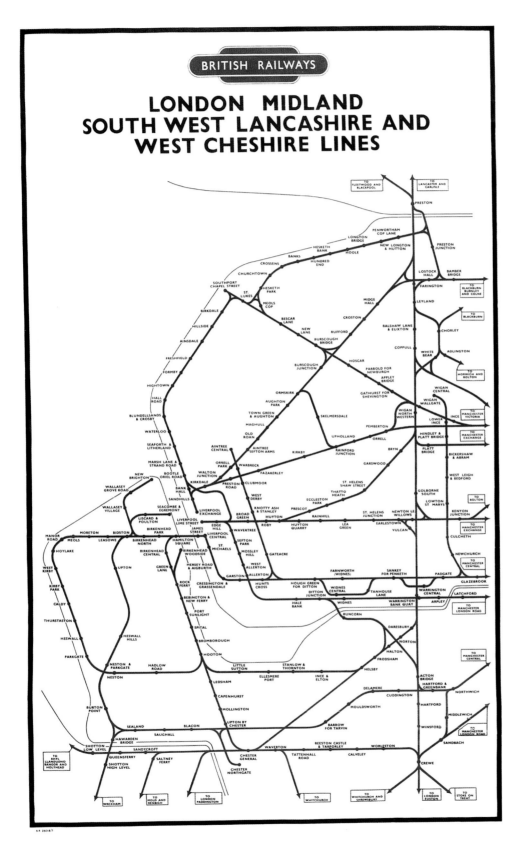

6.16 Complexity in the industrial north west: South West Lancashire and West Cheshire Lines. BR 35018/7

Stan Friedman collection

6.17 Possibly too complex to be successful, but a geographic map would have been even more difficult: South East Lancashire and Manchester Lines. BR 35018/5

Stan Friedman collection

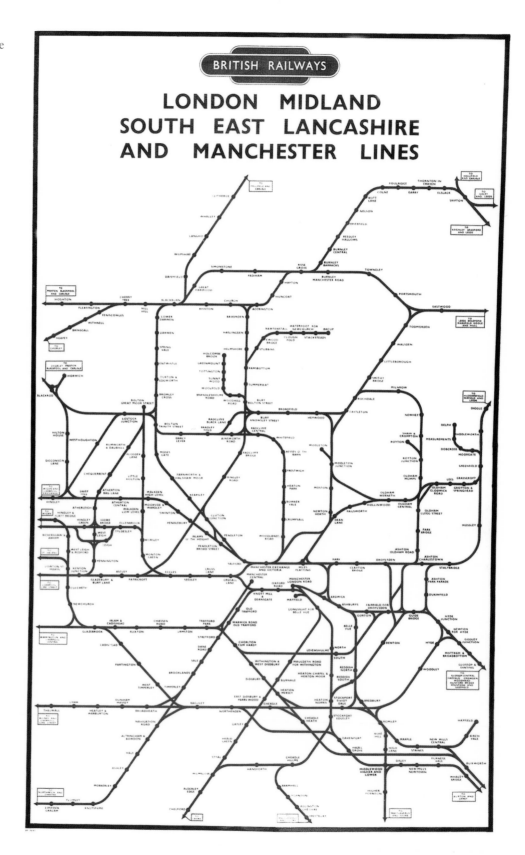

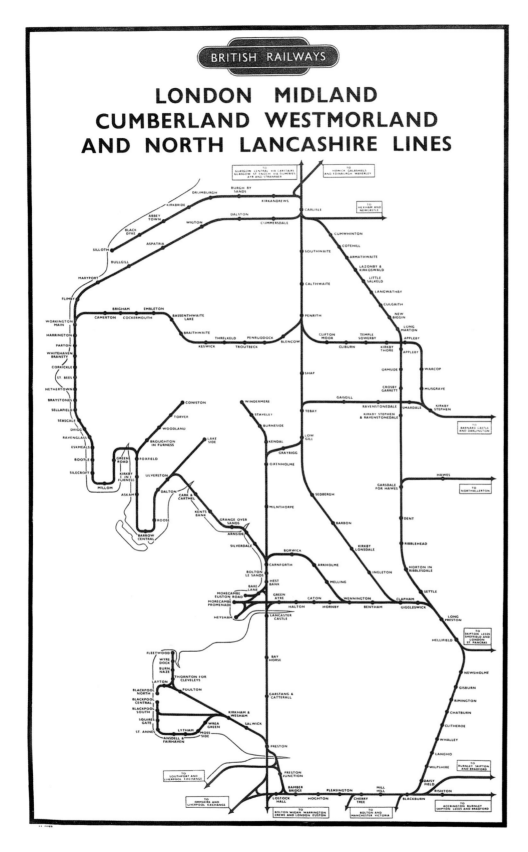

6.18 Cumberland Westmorland
and North Lancashire Lines.
BR 35018/8

Stan Friedman collection

6.19 The other was simplified by having fewer crossing lines: St Pancras and Euston Lines. It showed facilities near stations, *à la* LNER suburban map, from pre-war days. No ERO number.

Stan Friedman collection

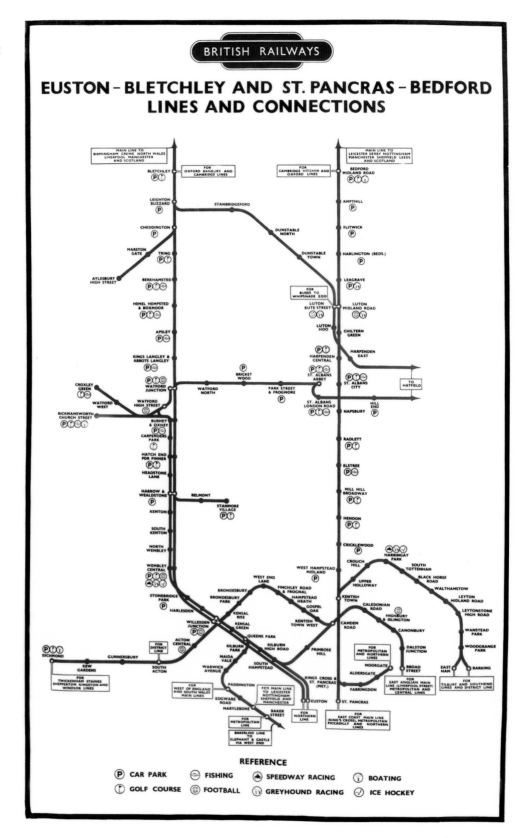

The un-numbered map referred to earlier showed the Euston–Bletchley and St Pancras–Bedford Lines, as on BR 35018/10, albeit re-drawn to a slightly different layout [6.19]. Most interesting is the addition of pictograms to show car parks and sporting venues near the stations. The idea was straight from the LNER London Suburban Dowagram of 1938.

In 1955 George Dow moved on again, this time into the Commercial organisation and away from direct responsibility for public relations. By then, the diagrammatic map was well established. The London Underground map was well on its way to becoming a design icon, and adopted as a model by metropolitan railway systems all over the world[15] – in the case of Sydney, as early as 1939. The Southern Railway, carrying such huge numbers every day, had as great a need for simplified maps as any other. They used a diagrammatic map on the rear cover of electric services pocket timetables in 1938[16], but none in its other main line timetables. The LMS, which had made limited use of diagrammatic maps with George Dow's assistance, seemed not to absorb the idea as much as it might have, and for many years clung to the basic simplified geographical map used by the Midland Railway for its timetables. The Great Western toyed with some inelegant diagrammatic area maps in 1934 and later, in brochures for rover tickets. But other than these, there is no evidence that the Great Western, which had little suburban traffic, had any wish to use them at all, even though its GW & GC line from Paddington had been included in the GC lines map of the LNER Dowagram in 1932.

George Dow's direct involvement with railway public relations ended in 1955. His last professional involvement with maps was a geographical map of the London Midland Region's lines, produced on a mirror which was placed in main line compartments. He continued to draw maps, as he always had: the four commemorative histories he had written for the LNER each had a map that he had drawn; five of his other books contained maps from his pen (the history of the Great Central contained 27 maps and 8 gradient diagrams); and he drew maps for three railway histories published by Ian Allan[17]. When his early maps for the LNER and others are included, the tally, geographical and diagrammatic, ran to over eighty in number.

15. In his book *Metro Maps of the World*, Mark Ovendon defines Metropolitan systems as those "planned or built as a segregated subterranean network." This definition may satisfy some purposes, but it is a fact that many main line railway companies have substantial suburban railway operations but not underground. The most significant of these are probably the lines of the former Southern Railway (and Southern Region of British Railways) in Great Britain, and the Long Island Railroad in the United States. Further, any definition of a metropolitan railway which excludes the Pacific Electric Railway, around which modern Los Angeles was built, or the Liverpool Overhead Railway, is courageous indeed.

16. Including a spelling mistake in one of the station names, West Weybridge.

17. The second edition of Hamilton Ellis's Midland Railway history, after George Dow had commented upon the poor map (by Ellis) at the back of the first edition; Cecil J Allen's *Great Eastern Railway*, London, 1955; and Hamilton Ellis' *North British Railway*, London, 1955.

73

7. The evolution of the diagrammatic railway map

It is clear that the main line railway companies had used diagrammatic presentation of maps for internal purposes, such as the signal box map and the depiction of gradients, for many years before the device of the simplified, stylised map was used for public purposes. In the forms used by railway companies for public purposes, the modern diagrammatic map evolved into widespread acceptance over a period of about thirty years: it was not the product of a single inventive mind, nor was it confined only to metropolitan railways.

The development of the modern diagrammatic map was spurred in different ways for different purposes. The main line companies, which demonstrably took the lead, used it to attract attention to initiatives in ticketing and to newly electrified services; a small number of diagrammatic or semi-diagrammatic maps appeared on posters. The Great Central appears to have been the first British company to use a simple diagrammatic map, to tell of the applicability of a cheap weekly season ticket, in 1904. The Lancashire & Yorkshire Railway appears to have been first in identifying a need for dedicated route maps within rolling stock. It did this on its newly electrified services between Liverpool and Southport, probably from the start in 1904. Then and later, electrification of a line previously operated by steam traction was often the spur to the use of simplified (meaning in this case "modern") means of presenting information.[1] This was largely because the main line companies had virtually ceased building new lines by this time, but it is probable that they would have used modern diagrammatic maps to present new lines to the public had they built them.

The main line companies made only limited use of diagrammatic maps in trains, primarily because of the slow pace of electrification. There was no incentive to use a dedicated route map in a steam-hauled carriage that might be used on any one of several routes within a company. Some companies which electrified lines appear not to have realised the benefits to be obtained from a dedicated route map, even though the circumstances were right for its application; the most ardent electrifier, the Southern Railway, used rolling stock with wide route availability on its electrified lines.[2]

The London Underground companies, on the other hand, which identified a similar need for new, slick, means of presenting information to their passengers, were still developing their systems. They were quite quick in taking up the idea of the dedicated route map and had a great need to exploit it. These railways all had self-contained routes, and did not interchange rolling stock.[3] Electrification of their lines had long since taken place, and they used the diagrammatic map on new lines, and extensions of existing lines. It was for this reason that the continuous upgrading of route maps and posters was necessary, and the designers of the route maps used

1. Just as the L&Y used it in 1904, so the Southern Railway produced one of its very few diagrammatic maps when the West Sussex electrification was completed in 1938.

2. The LMS and LNER inherited isolated electrified lines, and these were supplemented by others, such as the MSJ&A in Manchester. The Great Western remained aloof from such things.

3. This is still true today.

in Underground trains were frequently required to revise them as new stations were opened.

It appears that after some experimentation, the London Underground companies adopted the diagrammatic route map in trains more widely in about 1920, if the dates of available photographs are a reliable guide to their introduction. Once they had done so, they used a substantially common style of diagrammatic map to great effect. The designers of the maps are not known, but the similarity of most points of style, including the use of Johnston's typeface, suggests either the use of a single artist, or at least some level of co-ordination between the companies.

Because the railway diagrammatic map evolved, it is not possible to say that a particular map was the first. The District Railway route diagram of 1908, in principle, and the Bakerloo poster of 1908, in style, were very close to the form later adopted by London Underground as a whole, but we must not fall into the trap of thinking that the familiar London Underground map is the only form that a diagrammatic map could or should take. The Bakerloo 1908 poster was not the first and its appearance was almost incidental: it was designed to illustrate attractions, with the map, such as it was, placed in the available spaces between the rectangular illustrations of places and attractions. The lines served to hang the attractions together, seeking to attract custom but not to serve as directions for the passenger, and the use of such a simplified device was comprehensively ignored by the Underground companies for many years.[4] It appears, however, that the first widespread and systematic use of unquestionably diagrammatic maps was in about 1919 or 1920, following closely the ideas laid down in the Bakerloo map of 1908.

It certainly appears that while the early uses of diagrammatic presentation were confined to route diagrams, showing a single line of route, the 1929 LNER diagrams showed entire systems; this was the forward leap necessary to introduce the diagram into far more extensive, complex and intense maps than hitherto, and from that time the diagrammatic map has known no bounds. In this, the LNER was not only ahead of London Underground, but also ahead of Berlin, which produced its first diagrammatic system map in 1931.

There is no doubt that H. C. Beck, with his 1933 and subsequent maps of the London Underground system, made a significant contribution to the understanding of the capital's railways [7.1]. But it is clear that most or all of the eight lines that made up the Underground system at that time were already represented in individual diagrammatic route maps, and that Beck was familiar with at least some of them. In creating his map in 1931–33, he drew these diagrams together, arranging them to ensure comprehension and coherence, and did so using established diagrammatic mapping techniques, applying them to the entire LU system for the first time. Reference to the table on page 77 will make it clear that all of these

4. It is for this reason that the 1908 Bakerloo map has not featured any more extensively in the table on page 77 as the first detected use of that most fundamental diagrammatic feature, the straight line. Indeed, the first straight line map was probably a line in the sand, in prehistoric times. But this should not detract from the importance of the 1908 map in the evolution that we are examining.

7.1 The Henry Beck London Underground map as first published in January 1933. By this date, all of the London Underground lines were using diagrammatic route maps in their trains, and were slowly working towards standard symbology. With the use of ticks for stations and diamonds for interchanges, this map increased the number of cartographic devices in use by London Underground. The map relied heavily upon colour for coherence, but this was one of its major attractions.

London's Transport Museum

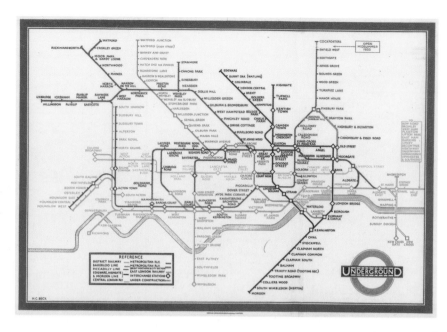

5. In *Mr Beck's Underground Map*, Ken Garland said that Beck was an electrician, accustomed to wiring diagrams, and states that such diagrams may have inspired the map. This is not a convincing argument and does not explain why, from the start, H. C. Beck used well-established diagrammatic conventions, many of which were developed by predecessors of his own employer, in his first map.

6. London's Transport Museum collection of route diagrams from cars is so sparse that it is not possible to tell whether or not co-ordination of map and style changes in those diagrams was co-ordinated with changes to the Beck map after the latter was introduced. The chances are that they were not, until many years later.

7. For example, the LNER London all lines Suburban Map, which appeared pasted in the back of the appropriate timetables, was modified in 1947 to remove the line through Stapleford and Watton-at-Stone, between Hertford and Stevenage. British Railways had it redrawn to reflect the transfer of branches to LT.

cartographic devices were already in existence and available to H. C. Beck.[5] He was then fortunate in the system's need for continual review of the total map, as lines were extended, because this gave him an opportunity not only to be associated with the map over a long period but also time to experiment with new cartographic devices, and to bring some of the other established devices to bear on the map.[6]

The main line companies did not have a need for continuous development, although occasionally the reverse was true, as line closures or discontinuance of service required changes to maps.[7] These imperatives notwithstanding, the LNER and LMS did make contributions to the arts and sciences of diagrammatic map design, and it will have been noticed in earlier chapters that much of the lead in the stylistic development of the diagrammatic map took place more often in route diagrams displayed in rolling stock than in posters at the station. Indeed, it can be argued that the route diagram was the principal vehicle for many of the features of diagrammatic design development.

With the appearance of its three route diagrams in 1929 and 1932, the LNER was ahead of its contemporaries in applying the diagrammatic map to the whole of its London suburban services. At that time, it can be seen that the diagrammatic map had reached a new level of discipline, not least because two maps with the same cartographic devices were issued simultaneously, which is more than one can observe with contemporaneous Underground route diagrams. Indeed in 1929 the diagrammatic map had matured, and only required stylistic refinement to make it universally acceptable as a valid means of rapid conveyance of information to travellers.

With the LNER maps, George Dow recognised the fact that the majority of the passengers on the lines were travelling to and from big

London termini. There had to be a sense of route or of line, to and from these stations, because that was what those railways were about. But with the London Underground, the termini, most of which were out in the country, played a much smaller role, and passengers were, in the main, travelling between intermediate stations on a system that, taken as a whole, covered an area rather than lines of route.

The essential and stylistic characteristics of the modern diagrammatic map can be seen to have emerged thus:

Feature[8]		date	where found
Route maps			
In-carriage dedicated route map[9]		c.1904	LYR Liverpool–Southport line
In-carriage dedicated diagrammatic route map		c.1908	District Railway
Lines			
Straight lines	minor	1904	Great Central weekly ticket poster
	extensive	c. 1904	City & South London Railway
Coloured lines		1908	LU system map
Casing (twin lines) for other companies' routes		1929	LNER GN and GE Lines route diagrams
Vertical lines		1920	Hampstead route diagram[10]
		1929	LNER GE Lines route diagram[11]
Horizontal lines		c. 1904	Central London map
		c. 1908	District Line route diagram
45-degree lines		1921	*possibly* District route diagram[12]
Parallel lines		1920	Hampstead route diagram
Lines of common angle		1929	LNER GE Lines route diagram
Stations			
Equally-spaced		1904	L&Y Liverpool–Southport route map
		1904	Great Central weekly ticket map
Distinction between ordinary stations and interchange		1908	Underground
	Interchange – ring	1908	Underground
	Interchange – white line connector	1909	London Electric
		1935	LMS Tilbury lines – first diagrammatic use
Diamond symbols for stations		1921	Met. route diagram
External tick for stations			
	(double sided)	1889	Met. Rly. map
	(single-sided)	1898	Met. Rly. map
Internal tick for stations		c. 1918	Great Northern all-line maps in timetables
Connection details in flags		1916	Piccadilly route diagram
Attractions in flags		1931	MSJ&A diagrammatic route map
Station names			
Preference for station names on the same side of the line		1904	L&YR route diagram
In colour to designate interchange		c. 1908	District Line route diagram
Station names all horizontal		c. 1908	District Line route diagram
Use of lower case in station names		1936	LNER Advertising Map
System			
Coverage of entire system		1929	LNER GN & GE Lines route diagrams
Predominance of geometric symmetry		1936	LNER London Suburban map

The diagrammatic railway map as we understand it today is dominated by straight lines, and by a limited number of angles at which those lines are set. The shape of many cities, and the railways that serve them, lead the map designer towards the use of vertical, horizontal, and 45 degree lines only, simply because the symmetry of these three allows a sense of shape and direction to be maintained. But, as we can see in the huge variety of railway maps illustrated in Mark Ovendon's *Metro Maps of the*

8. This list must be regarded as tentative, because further maps may be found which set dates earlier.

9. As distinct from entire system.

10. Very short, between two stations.

11. Substantial use on formal map

12. The Palace Gates branch on the LNER GE lines map of 1929 is most certainly at 45 degrees.

World, maps do not have to obey all of these conventions to be successful. Equally it can be seen that diagrammatic presentation does not of itself guarantee success.

The table above could, no doubt, be extended to incorporate developments since the War, but it can be argued that by that time, or possibly 1937, when George Dow created his predominantly diagonal LNER London area map complete with symbols for local attractions, the British diagrammatic map can be seen to have come of age, and to have become a wholly acceptable means of presenting information to the city traveller. It certainly seems that in this development Britain led the world, and it was from about this time that other cities showed, through the issuance of their own maps, how influential this British development was becoming. It may be that the London Underground diagrammatic map was the most exposed of all, simply because it covered so much of London, but it can also be seen that the LU style of map was not the only style developed before the war, nor necessarily the only standard to follow.

The London Underground map remained in H. C. Beck's hands for several years, although not exclusively. It is interesting that in 1940 LT developed a new version of the map in which the diagonals were reduced to a very few, perhaps following the lead from George Dow's 1935 poster map for the LMS, albeit not at a rakish angle. For the next twenty-two years the Beck map remained in this style, and arguably this reduction of geography to geometry could be seen to have gone too far: the layout had become too mechanical and had overwhelmed any sense of direction for the casual user. While it was true that seasoned users of the Underground could remind themselves very easily of how to make their journeys, visitors may not have found it so easy. In 1964 the map was returned to a form far closer to H. C. Beck's original design, and it has remained thus ever since.

British Railways and its successors made extensive use of the diagrammatic map, in various forms, just as have railway administrations all over the world, but in retrospect it can be seen that while styles have increased in their variety, the diagrammatic map has not been changed in its essentials since the 1930s. Illustrated here is a map of the territory of Arriva Trains Northern, which in all essentials save the open rings for the stations follows the style of the Welch/Dow area maps of the London Midland Region fifty years ago [7.1]. It shows that the London Underground map, although much admired, is not the only standard to which contemporary map designers aspire.

It is not known if George Dow and H. C. Beck ever met, and it is not possible to know with certainty the extent to which the work of each influenced the other. It cannot be stated categorically that H. C. Beck was influenced by George Dow's 1929 maps, but it would be remarkable if as a resident of Highgate, on the LNER system, he never saw them.[13] It is not

13. If Beck never saw the LNER GN Lines map, it was indeed a remarkable coincidence that Beck used the same device - casing - to indicate the GN & City line from Finsbury Park to Moorgate. He also used it to show the East London Railway, until July 1933 leased to a Joint Committee, in which shares were held by the District, Metropolitan, LNER and the Southern. LPTB took over responsibility for operation on 1 July that year. Thereafter the only line in external ownership shown on LU maps was the Waterloo & City Line (from 1937) until BR's Crossrail routes appeared in 1994, again shown by the same device.

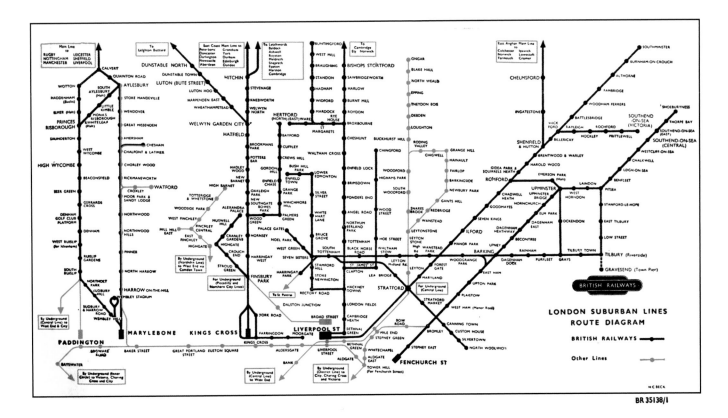

BR 35138/1

possible that Beck was unaware of route diagrams in the Underground trains that he is stated to have used between his workplace and home. In later years he had to fight for recognition of his right to develop his map (as he saw it) and it is suggested that in these circumstances he was not likely to admit of any external influence in its conception. To have done so would have been to admit the simple fact that he was merely one of a number of participants in an evolutionary process.[14] George Dow, naturally very observant, was bound to have noticed the route diagrams that he saw each working day,[15] and although he used the forty-five degree line in 1929, he may have been influenced by Beck's fondness for it once he could get out of the strait-jacket of the compartment display. It is equally possible, though, that he had always wanted to use it more extensively, and needed no prompting. The forty-five degree line is very important to the symmetry of a more or less square map, and he used it to exceptionally good effect in his LNER London Suburban maps of 1936 and 1937.

There is a postscript to these LNER maps. After nationalisation, when the Ongar branch of the LNER had been progressively taken over by London Transport, and when the Eastern Region of British Railways wanted a new version of the old LNER map, they commissioned H. C. Beck to produce it [7.2]. He followed George Dow's layout closely, but he detached the GC lines and showed them vertically, thus destroying the symmetry of the map.[16] Had there been any form of cartographic etiquette

7.2 Beck's only known commission for British Railways was this, for the Eastern Region. It was based upon George Dow's earlier map for the LNER, but without the symmetry.

Peter Lloyd collection

14. Perhaps it would be uncharitable to suggest also that for this reason the claim that circuit diagrams inspired the first Beck map was attractive.

15. He acknowledged this in his lecture *Twenty-one Years with the LNER*, prepared in the 1970s.

16. This was done when Beck was well into what has erroneously been called "rectilinear" presentation. By this was meant presentation largely by vertical and horizontal lines. Beck abandoned the extensive use of diagonals in 1941. He had used prominent diagonals for only eight years, and remained with dominant verticals and horizontals for the next eighteen. His treatment of the Eastern Region London Suburban map was merely another application of this form of layout.

in those days, this surgery on a fellow map-maker's design would no doubt have been regarded as rather bad form. As we have seen in the case of the 1933 Underground map, this was not the first instance of H. C. Beck relying heavily on the earlier work of others for his own output.[17]

Both men have handed down to us a fine tradition of map design. They both contributed to the evolution of the railway diagrammatic map as we know it today, using elements developed along the way, but in the much-admired first London Underground map of 1933 it is difficult to find any cartographic device that is entirely new. Its attraction lay in its new combination of a number of essential and stylistic elements, not least of which were the use of the 45-degree line, and the use of colour.[18]

George Dow showed considerable adaptability in his work, in continuing to design a variety of diagrammatic maps of various systems for the LNER, as well as for the LMS. These were of many differing styles and of high quality, and he was much flattered by *The Railway Gazette* having coined the word *Dowagram* to describe his distinctive work. He clearly was a disciple of the diagrammatic map, as can be seen from the extent to which he introduced it to the London Midland Region, in the event far more extensively than he had ever done for the LNER. But by then he was the commissioner, not the commissioned, and he had significant responsibility to discharge in keeping the Region's passengers well informed in every way.

In later years George Dow said little about his role in the evolution of the diagrammatic map, but there is little doubt that he contributed a great deal. To him they were but a small part of what he had done in a very busy career and a very busy life. His wider achievements in railway public relations, his work as a railway historian, and his devotion to railways as the most civilised form of transport were all, in his view, at least as significant as his efforts with maps. But that is not to say that his work on maps was unimportant. Not only was he ahead of Beck in nearly all of the innovations which established the diagrammatic map in the form in which we know it today, but he was directly and closely associated with maps of several systems while Beck only dealt with two.[19] Perhaps, indeed, we can see influences from his work in some of the many maps in use today. The fact that five of George Dow's original diagrammatic designs were printed straight from his artwork underlines his skills of cartography and layout. The work *was* important to him, for he kept a copy of all but one of the designs he had created; without that record this brief account would have been all the more difficult to compile.

17. It is not known if the Eastern Region approached George Dow to ask him to redraw his LNER map. By late 1949 he was a senior officer on the London Midland Region and although the Eastern Region (particularly the Commercial Superintendent, Cecil Dandridge) knew him well, it was probably assumed that he would not have had time to devote to it. Equally, as LT was the beneficiary of the transfer of lines, it is possible that they offered Beck's services to produce the new map.

18. When *The Railway Gazette* reproduced the Beck map, in July 1933, it was printed in black and white, which emphasised its need for colour to be understood, and much of its impact was thus lost. The magazine referred to the design, without any accompanying paragraph, as "modernist".

19. As well as his work for the Eastern Region of BR, Beck volunteered a design for the Paris Metro, which was not accepted.

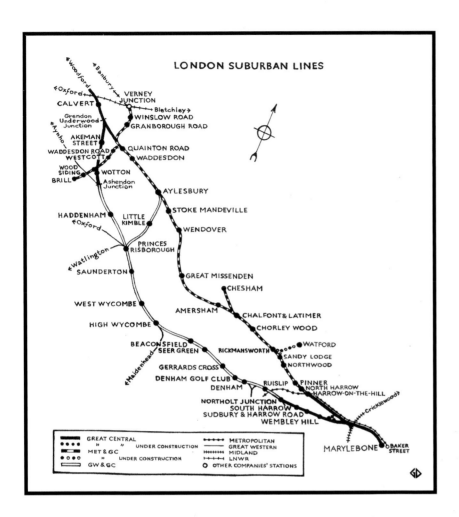

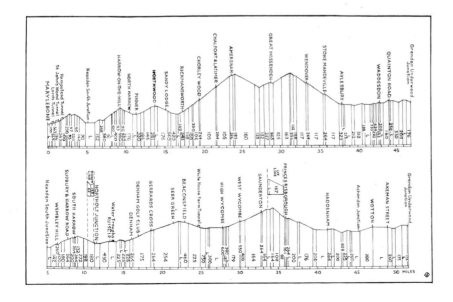

7.3 George Dow's involvement with maps continued for many years. Within his *magnum opus*, the three-volume *Great Central* he prepared many maps and diagrams. Included were a geographical map of the lines from Marylebone, showing the two routes by which the GC reached London, and...

7.4 ... a gradient diagram of the two routes. The only signal box diagrams that he drew were for the family model railway.

7.5 The Welch/Dow style of area map lives! Arriva Trains Northern map of October 2002.

Arriva Trains Northern

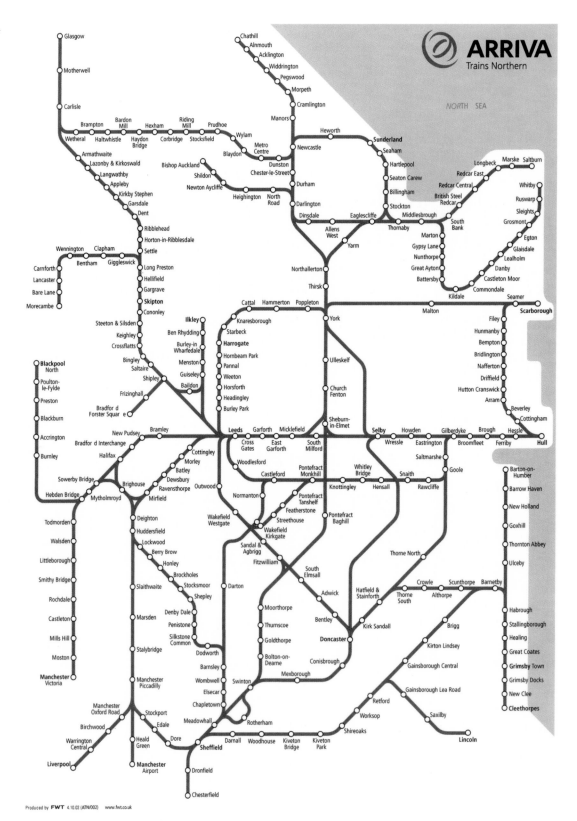

Appendix
Diagrammatic maps by George Dow

	Subject	*date*	*Lines included*
	LNER, LMS, and others		
1	**GN suburban lines** LNER, hand-drawn carriage panel Black and red on white card 20″ × 10″	1929	King's Cross, Moorgate and Broad Street to Edgware, Hertford, St Albans, Dunstable and Stevenage
2	**GE suburban lines** LNER hand-drawn carriage panel Black and red on white card 20″ × 10″	1929	Liverpool Street, Fenchurch Street and Gospel Oak to Enfield Town, Chingford, Ongar, Southend, Beckton and North Woolwich
3	**MSJ&A** LMS hand-drawn carriage panel Black on cream card 24″ × 10″ Manchester at right (BR version had Manchester at left)	1931	Manchester London Road to Altrincham & Bowdon
4	**GC suburban lines** LNER, typeset (Gill Sans) carriage panel Black and red on white card 20″ × 10″	1932	Marylebone, Liverpool Street and Paddington to Verney Jct, Calvert, Brill, Chesham and Watford
5	**Shenfield Widening** Hand-drawn diagram to show widening of lines	1933	Liverpool Street to Shenfield
6	**Tilbury & Southend Lines** LMS hand-drawn carriage panel Black and red on cream card 21¾″ × 8¾″ and 25″ × 10″	1935	Fenchurch Street and St Pancras to Romford, Tilbury and Shoeburyness
7	**London suburban electric lines** LMS hand-drawn poster Double Royal	1935	Euston, Broad Street and Poplar to Watford Jct, Croxley Green, Rickmansworth and Clapham
8	**LNER London all suburban lines** Typeset (Gill Sans); for commercial advertisers Black and red on white paper 15½″ × 13″, folded	1936	King's Cross, Marylebone, Liverpool Street, Fenchurch Street to Huntington, Brackley, Cambridge Ongar, Chelmsford, Southend etc
9	**LNER London suburban lines for timetables** Typeset, based closely on item 7, but with much added data on facilities at and near stations Black and blue on white paper, as item 7	1937	As item 8, but also showing timetable numbers adjacent to lines
9a	**LNER London suburban lines for timetables**	1946	As item 9 but with revisions of symbols (e.g. parking added at Cambridge, deleted at Quainton Road.) Timetable numbers omitted
9b	**LNER London suburban lines for timetables**	1947	As item 9 but all activity symbols deleted. LPTB lines highlighted. Basic layout unchanged except for minor revisions and deletion of line from Hertford North to Stevenage; also deletion of line from Woodham Ferrers to Maldon. Deletion of reference to design by George Dow
10	**Tyneside electric route diagram** LNER, typeset carriage panel Black and red on white card 30″ × 10″	1938	Newcastle Central to Tynemouth (three routes) and South Shields
11	**Tyneside electric route diagram** LNER, typeset carriage panel, as item 9	1938	As 10 but no South Shields line
12	**Grimsby & Immingham** LNER, typeset map in brochure	1938	All-line LNER map and shipping routes to northern Europe.
13	**Hull** LNER, typeset map in brochure	1939	All-line LNER map and shipping routes to northern Europe.
14	**London** Hand-drawn for newspaper.	1941	To support proposals (in accompanying article published in *The Star* 14 June 1941) for cross-London tunnels and new main line stations, post war.

Official publications

London Midland and Eastern Regions
Commemorative booklet for the opening of the newly electrified Manchester - Sheffield - Wath lines in 1954. The booklet was produced under the joint names of the ER and LMR, but followed the style of contemporary LM booklets. At the back, tipped in, was a diagrammatic map of the electrified lines.

(i)   **Electrified lines, Manchester-Sheffield-Wath**
          1954
          typeset

While PR & PO of the London Midland Region, 1949-1955, George Dow commissioned a number of diagrammatic maps relevant to services on the LM. The maps were designed under his guidance (and referring to his earlier examples) by a member of his staff, Vic Welch. A tentative list is:

London Midland Region
Carriage panel route maps:
(a) (i) **Euston, Broad Street, Watford and Richmond lines**
        Typeset carriage panel, black and red on white card 20″ × 10″.
        Probably a prototype: all other LM diagrams had a black border; no ERO or BR reference number.

(a) (ii) **Euston, Broad Street, Watford and Richmond lines**
        Typeset carriage panel, black and red on white card 20″ × 10″.
        Revised layout, to include Rickmansworth and to avoid suggestion Euston is on a branch. Examples may be seen in the Oerlikon vehicle preserved at National Railway Museum.
        ERO 53226/6

(a) (iii) **Euston, Broad Street, Watford and Richmond lines**
        Typeset carriage panel, black and red on white paper 54″ × 12″
        Does not include Rickmansworth, but Euston is on a branch.
        BR 35019/18

(a) (iv) **Euston, Broad Street, Watford and Richmond lines**
        As above; second version with flagged information in Gills Sans Medium
        BR 35019/18

(b)   **Manchester and Altrincham line**
        Typeset carriage panel, black and red on white card 25″ × 10″
        ERO 53226-4

(c)   **Lancaster Morecambe and Heysham Electric lines**
        Typeset carriage panel, black and red on white paper 24″ × 9¼″
        BR 35019/19

(d)   **Manchester Glossop and Hadfield lines**
        Typeset carriage panel, black and red on white paper 45″ × 9″
        (no reference number)

(e) (i) **Liverpool Southport and Ormskirk lines**
        Typeset carriage panel, black and red on white paper 24″ × 9″
        ERO 53226-5

(e) (ii) **Liverpool Southport and Ormskirk lines**
        Typeset carriage panel, black and red on white paper 24″ × 9″
        Revised version to delete the connecting line between Aintree and Marsh Lane & Strand Road.
        ERO 53226-5

(f) (i) **Mersey and Wirral lines**
        Typeset carriage panel, black and red on white paper 60″ × 10½″
        ERO 53226-3

(f) (ii) **Mersey and Wirral lines**
        Second version with deletion of reference to Storeton as a destination from Bidston
        Typeset carriage panel, black and red on white paper 60″ × 10½″
        ERO 53226-3

(f) (iii) **Mersey and Wirral lines**
        Smaller version of first, minor changes to layout
        Typeset carriage panel, black and red on white paper 29½″ × 10½″
        ERO 53226-2

Handed pair:
(g) (i) (a) **Manchester and Bury line**
        Manchester Victoria at right
        Typeset carriage panel, black and red on white paper 26″ × 9½″
        Reference to Bolton connection at Radcliffe Central
        ERO 53577/10

(g) (i) (b) **Manchester and Bury line**
        Manchester Victoria at left
        Typeset carriage panel, black and red on white paper 26″ × 9½″
        Reference to Bolton connection at Radcliffe Central
        ERO 53577/10

(g) (ii) **Manchester and Bury line**
        Manchester Victoria at left
        Typeset carriage panel, black and red on white paper 26″ × 9½″
        No reference to Bolton connection at Radcliffe Central
        ERO 53577/14

(g) (iii) **Manchester Bury and Holcombe Brook line**
        Manchester Victoria at left
        Typeset carriage panel, black and red on white paper 35″ × 9½″
        Reference to Bolton connection at Radcliffe Central
        Shows route as in /10 above but runs on to Holcombe Brook
        ERO 53226-1

Double Royal Posters:
(h)   **North Wales Lines**
        Typeset double royal poster for display at stations.
        BR 35018/1

(i)   **Bedford Rugby Coventry and Northampton District Lines**
        Typeset double royal poster for display at stations.
        BR 35018/2

(j)   **South Staffordshire and Birmingham Lines**
Typeset double royal poster for display at stations.
BR 35018/3

(k)   **North Staffordshire and South Cheshire Lines**
Typeset double royal poster for display at stations.
BR 35018/4

(l)   **South East Lancashire and Manchester Lines**
Typeset double royal poster for display at stations.
BR 35018/5

(m)   **Derby Leicester and Nottingham Lines**
Typeset double royal poster for display at stations.
BR 35018/6

(n)   **South West Lancashire and West Cheshire Lines**
Typeset double royal poster for display at stations.
BR 35018/7

(o)   **Cumberland Westmorland and North Lancashire Lines**
Typeset double royal poster for display at stations.
BR 35018/8

(p)   *Title not established*
Presumably a typeset double royal poster for display at stations.
BR 35018/9

(q)   **London Suburban Lines**
Typeset double royal poster for display at stations.
BR 35018/10

(r)   **St Pancras and Euston Lines**
Typeset double royal poster for display at stations. No ERO number
Embodies attraction/facility symbols in the style of 9 above.

Bibliography

Barker, T C and Michael Robbins, *A History of London Underground*, Vol 2, London: George Allen & Unwin Ltd, 1974.

Barman, Christian, *The Man Who Built London Transport*, Newton Abbot: David & Charles, 1979.

Crump, Spencer, *Ride the Big Red Cars*, Glendale, California: Trans-Anglo Books, 1983.

Dow, George, *Twenty-one years with the LNER*, (unpublished script of talk), c. 1970

Garland Ken, *Mr Beck's Underground Map*, London: Capital Transport Publishing, 1994

Klapper, Charles, *London's Lost Railways*, London: Routledge & Kegan Paul, 1976.

Leboff, David and Tim Demuth, *No Need to Ask!*, London: Capital Transport Publishing, 1999

Moss, Paul, *Underground Movement*, London: Capital Transport Publishing, 2000

Official Guide, The, New York: The National Railway Publication Company, March 1937

Overton, Andrew, *Metro Maps of the World*, London: Capital Transport Publishing, 2003

Railway Gazette, London, various dates

Railway Magazine, The, London, various dates

Roberts, Maxwell J, *Underground Maps After Beck*, London: Capital Transport Publishing, 2005

Timetables, LNER, LMS, GWR and SR public timetables, various dates

Charles Wilson, *Harwich and the Continent*, London & North Eastern Railway, 1947.

Index

Illustrations are shown in bold numbers
Footnotes (and numbers where necessary) are shown as suffixes to page numbers, e.g. 27n19